THE POLITICAL ECONOMY OF INDIA'S FOREIGN POLICY

RADHARAMAN CHAKRABARTI

Institute of
Foreign Policy Studies
(IFPS)

Centre for Pakistan
and West Asian Studies
(CPWAS)

Calcutta University
Kolkata

in association with

KNOWLEDGE WORLD

KW Publishers Pvt Ltd
New Delhi

The Court of Directors of the East India Company sent a despatch in July, 1854 to the Governor-General of India in Council, suggesting the establishment of the Universities of Calcutta, Madras and Bombay. In pursuance of that despatch, the University of Calcutta was founded on January 24, 1857. The University adopted in the first instance, the pattern of the University of London and gradually introduced modifications in its constitution.

The Institute of Foreign Policy Studies (IFPS) at the University of Calcutta is an autonomous centre devised for the study of international relations, with particular emphasis on foreign policy. Funded by the Ministry of External Affairs (MEA), Government of India, the institute purports to create a pool of foreign policy specialists capable of offering advice on matters pertaining to India's international relations. The Institute has already been earmarked for developing regional expertise with reference to the Government of India's Look East Policy, and that towards West Asia. The IFPS has also been chosen as one of the ten centres for United Nations Academic Initiative, functioning as the hub for studies on peace and conflict resolution.

The Centre for Pakistan and West Asian Studies (CPWAS), Calcutta University, was set up in 2005 under the UGC Area Studies Programme. It is the only research outfit associated with a University in eastern India with an exclusive focus on Pakistan and West Asian countries, Afghanistan, Iran and Iraq in particular, which together constitute a part of India's extended neighbourhood in the West. The Centre, since its establishment in 2005, has tried to develop a greater understanding of this extended neighbourhood by looking at the internal dynamics of the region with far greater detail than is generally accorded by other area studies outfits in the country.

The First Edition was published in 1982 by KP Bagchi & Company, Calcutta.

ISBN 978-93-81904-92-3

Published in India by Kalpana Shukla

KNOWLEDGE WORLD
KW Publishers Pvt Ltd
4676/21, First Floor, Ansari Road, Daryaganj, New Delhi 110002
Phone: +91 11 23263498/43528107
Email: knowledgeworld@vsnl.net • www.kwpub.com

Printed and Bound in India

2011 FPBA BEST PUBLISHERS AWARD (ENGLISH)

To

Sukalpa, Avik and Krishna

for their rewarding company

at the time of writing the book

Contents

Introduction

(to the present Calcutta University Edition)

Nothing could be more rewarding to an author than witnessing reprint of a fairly old work of his and that too under the auspices of the premier University in this part of the world. I was singularly delighted when the Hon'ble Vice Chancellor of the University of Calcutta, Professor Suranjan Das, wanted my consent to get my work titled "The Political Economy of India's Foreign Policy" reprinted by the Institute of Foreign Policy Studies of the University. I took it as an honour to offer my instant and unconditional consent.

The work was the product of my post-doctoral research done at the University of Washington, Seattle, USA as an Indo-US Exchange Fellow (1978-79). At that time few foreign policy studies, and certainly none on India's foreign relations, were subjected to a full scale theoretical examination from the political economy angle. Notions of security, national interest, diplomatic leverage, decision making process etc were predominantly construed in terms of some inexorable power play. The domestic –external continuum too used to be hazily conceived. Internal constraints were, at the most, understood as institutional deficiency or as some inescapable human limitation on the part of the key decision makers. This made me take a critical look at the forces located both far and near that combined in varying strength to give a discernible direction to India's foreign policy drives.

The period covered in this work {early 1950s to early 1980s} saw the towering presence of at least two Prime Ministers at the helm of external as well as internal affairs, the defining moments of Non-alignment as a doctrine and as an activist stance, the turbulence of regional politics marked by armed conflicts, the shadow of a nuclear arms build-up close to the borders, a significant alteration of South Asian Balance of power, the expediency-led modification of an avowed posture of equidistance from the bipolar rivals and, of course, the deepening bonds offered by the Soviet bloc serving as an interesting contrast with the syndrome of "estranged democracies" which marked the greater part of Indo-US relations. Those were, essentially, political-ideological manifestations of an evolving foreign policy that had more deeply laid domestic economic forces and political agenda reflecting the legitimate aspirations of a great people that refused to be treated as some odd nation out in the international community. But then there was substantial hiatus between the aspiration and the capability aspects of policy, and it entailed the most challenging task of bringing the entire gamut of political economy to bear the desired outcome. Domestic economic management was to be so orchestrated as to get the maximum mileage out of the external milieu. It required not just an occasional master stroke but a stead-fast application of the economic instruments of policy, improvising and innovating all along, until the process could be mastered to the fullest extent. Whatever its direction, each policy move was expected to be consistent with the supreme goal of reducing national economic dependency so as to achieve substantial strength to back up an independent foreign policy stance.

On the face of it, the immediate area of operation would relate to foreign economic relations pertaining to trade, aid and investment., each requiring a careful balancing of advantages that could be extracted from the bipolar global economy. In practice, the Indian leadership was seized with a larger strategy to take the exercise far deeper so as to get interconnected with the expanding space in between the immediate preserve of the two poles of power. That space eminently belonged to the developing part of the world and it turned out to be a considerable space indeed. The objective was to serve the twin purposes of putting up a common platform vis-à-vis the prevailing hegemony and also to get the most out of a mutually sustained vision of economic advancement through coordination of external economic policies and maximizing the returns from existing complementarities. Though avowedly anti-hegemonic, it did not limit itself to mere anti-imperialist rhetoric, as is often suggested. On the contrary, a goal oriented agenda and a vigorous diplomatic drive to concretize the same characterized India's foreign policy making of this period. We are not concerned here with the internal tensions within the policy establishment or individual excellence of outstanding diplomats of which there were quite a few; nor are we caught up with the ideological trappings of a liberal democracy contending with alternative routes to the socialistic transformation of India. The principal focus of the study is on the policy design which simultaneously sought to synchronize domestic economic advancement with an assertive and autonomous position on vital issues of global and regional politics. Avowedly again, the tendency of big powers to build antagonistic alliance structures was disfavored. As against this there were conscious efforts by India at collectivization of policy outlooks of likeminded nations professing adherence to non-alignment which came to be regarded as the doctrinal portal of a vast multitude of developing nations. This would turn out in due course to be a support base for India while dealing with powers opposing its policies and legitimate interests. Economic partnership of various types reinforced this aggregated thrust, thereby creating an effective network for promotion of foreign policy objectives.

Clearly, therefore, an indigenous model was developed in which economic initiatives at home were synchronized with targeted expansion of commercial activities abroad, the fledgling private sector got the requisite orientation from a dominant public sector and politico-diplomatic resources were geared in a manner that national economic reconstruction and national foreign policy making went well in step with each other. The model made itself further interesting as it was pressed into service to serve a dual purpose i.e., not only to cope with the stressful bipolar structure of global politics but also to modify, in bits and pieces, the overall global order. The intended outcome was to reformulate the perceived "agent-structure" model, thereby making the agent less and less subservient to the command of the structure and gain in the process significant measure of autonomy in foreign policy application.

While the logic underlying the model is clear and its practicability has been tested on several occasions, the whole thing stood on a shifting relationship between an aspirant nation and the overall power construct then under near total dominance of the richer nations. What the aspirant nation in this model was seeking was substantive alteration of the dispensations of that power construct, obviously not by intimidation but by positioning itself at a vantage point where its claims would have legitimation of the majority of nations. A considerable range of such claims, through not all, had to be eventually conceded by the powers that be–be it the end of colonialism or racial repressions or a mitigation of unequal international terms of trade. Apart from these systemic changes, India also gained in her own favour certain advantages of market expansion, opportunities of inter-development initiatives with other growing nations and extracting donor aid at significantly concessional terms.

On the domestic front the apparent success of the aforementioned strategies produced mixed effects. On the one hand it largely increased the growth of the public sector's grip on the national economy, providing a useful range of alternatives to promote economic advancement. It also provided the much needed guidance for the private sector to test the waters of doing business with the socialist countries by virtue of state mediation, and they did gain much by way of diversification of their business. But then the grip of the public authorities was not to the liking of the self-serving entrepreneurial class of the country, although they owed a lot of their growth to continuous state patronage. They were just biding time when they and not the State would have the command and control of the economy. Early indications of this tension were in the offing in the eighties of last century, when the Indian State was visibly inclining towards a more relaxed regime so far as treatment of foreign investment was concerned. Consistent underperformance of the private sector and the constricted modus operandi of the public sector were steadily pushing the national economy to a downward slope. What followed during the next decade were only presaged by these trends, namely an acute foreign trade imbalance, a nagging depression, and uncontrollable fiscal deficit all leading to the near collapse of a more or less thriving economy under a nationally oriented public authority. This definitely affected the relationship of India's political economy with the global economic configuration and hence also its external political strategies but cannot be said to have put it on a critical trial until an unanticipated blow came with the collapse of the Soviet bloc, thus putting an abrupt end to the erstwhile polarities spaced out by a non-committal third world.

The present study did not come upto this stage which occurred towards the end of the nineties. As such the overall analysis was centred on the domestic and external milieu of the fifties to the eighties of the last century. But it did critique the viability of the basic framework of India's external relations once one or the other or even both underwent any vital change that would clearly put the policy maker face to face with a difficult choice, and a fundamentally revisionist choice at that, so far as the design of the domestic economy was concerned vis-à-vis a completely different world order rising from the post-Soviet, post-Cold War realities. The world suddenly took on a new, premillennial shake-up with the advent of Globalization — a multi-faceted phenomenon the essence of which lay in the acceptance of the market as the single most and nearly insuperable determinant of the global political economy to which the national economies were per force going to get integrated, India being no exception. The fact that India would no longer stand out as an exceptional actor spearheading a unique policy outlook was the inevitable outcome of the ideological transformation of the Indian political class, right-centre-and left. The ideological backlash of neo-liberalism of the West coupled with the strategic thrust of global capitalism captioned as "Washington Consensus" and the unipolar vision of successive American administrations since the Gulf War combined to floor much of the former zeal to build an appreciably pro-people nation state in the non-capitalist part of the world. Whatever was now left of the erstwhile foreign policy in the non-aligned mode had to undergo quick transformation, having but weak apologies to offer for the equations the South was eager to enter with the North.

The change of scenario has been as much significant as the response of nations like India. Obviously that called for a re-look into what led to the present state of affairs and also a critical assessment of the reconstruction of India's foreign policy under the new impulses of a market-driven, liberalized and globally oriented political economy. That has been the subject of my other, relatively recent work titled *India's External Relations in a Globalized World Economy* published by the Anthem Press under the auspices of the Maulana Abul Kalam Azad Institute of Asian Studies. Since that could as well be a companion volume to the present one, the decision of the University of Calcutta to bring the present work back into circulation may be taken as a welcome move, for which I am personally grateful to the Vice Chancellor of the University.

Kolkata
February 1, 2014 **Radharaman Chakrabarti**

Preface

The study was prompted by the recent awareness among experts in the field of International Politics of the need to analyse foreign policy of nations from an inter-disciplinary angle in which the tools of economic and political research reinforce each other. Indeed, the interdependence of economics and politics is so pronounced in today's world politics that a purely political approach to the understanding of foreign policy has not only become dated but calls for substantive modification in terms of the basic motivations which determine the foreign relations of nations.

In this context, India's foreign policy provides by far the most instructive instance of the innovative efforts of a nation to work out a foreign policy that has clear organic relations with a none too modest ambition of economic self –promotion. Practically speaking, Indian foreign policy with its emphasis on non-alignment and ascendancy of the third world politics is inextricably connected with the manifold programmes of economic development at home and restructuring foreign economic relations. For a newly independent country like India, foreign policy making has been essentially an art of making both ends meet, the economic and political. One of the major pre-occupations of foreign policy making in India consists in striking a balance between the resources of diplomacy and those of domestic economic development. Naturally the entire process has been one of trial and error, innovations, rejections and improvement. The methods that have been tried in this experiment, the hazards that have been encountered on the way and the social adjustments that have occurred in the process constitute the core of present enquiry.

The work begins with a preliminary quest for a feasible methodology of dealing with the subject delineated above. It then traces the major historical signposts that mark the evolution of an independent approach on the part of the Indian authorities to the problems of foreign policy making. The work then move on to explore the relationship between concepts of self-reliance, aid management, trade diversification and control of foreign investment and their relevance to the maintenance of an autonomous role in external affairs.

The study also takes into account the directions of business-government interaction in India since independence and the devices worked out so far a cautious coupling of internal and external capital within the broad frame work of a mixed economy. The entire exercise seems to have been based on an implicit consensus of the Indian business community in favour of the government's handling of the problems of foreign trade and foreign investment, including the operations of the powerful MNCs. At the same time one ought to notice how private Indian capital joins hand with state owned capital in an effort to branch forth into lucrative investments abroad, thereby engaging in a regular bridge-building operation with friendly third world countries. This phenomenon has been termed the art of 'inter developing' and is supposed to add a new economic dimension to the policy of non-alignment .In the concluding section a modest effort has been made to size up the potentiality of the policies so far pursued made by our decision makers and to make a tentative assessment of their cost-effectiveness.

The present work was undertaken as a post-doctoral research project which was facilitated by the award of a Visiting Fellowship by the University Grants Commission under the Indo-US Exchange programme for 1978-79.The project was completed in the most congenial academic environment of the University of Washington, Seattle, USA. I owe a profound debt of gratitude to my academic consultant Professor George Modelski, for the valuable suggestions he offered for the organisation and improvement of the monograph. The help rendered by the office staff and the library personnel in the University of Washington far exceeded my expectations and was really indispensable for completion of the work within the short span of one academic year. Valuable too was the benefit of discussions I had with the Faculty members, especially Professor Paul Brass and Dr Margaret Levi of Political Science department and Professor Frank F. Conlon of South Asian study center of the University of Washington.

I shall be failing in my duty if I did not mention the unique opportunity I had of meeting a galaxy of scholars from different parts of the world at the Annual Conference of Fulbright Scholars at the Washington International Center in March 1979. I must also acknowledge with thanks the great care taken by the Council for International Exchange of Scholars, Washington

D.C, for making our stay in the USA not only comfortable but really an enjoyable experience.

Needless to add that the work owes its completion mainly to the inspiring company of my family.

Back home I have been quite fortunate to come into contact with the reputed publishing concern, Messrs KP Bagchi of Calcutta, who have taken great plains to bring out the book in a remarkably short period of time.

I shall find my work amply rewarded if it can stimulate further and more equipped investigations in this relatively new field of study.

Calcutta
January 5,1982

Radharaman Chakrabarti

1
Why Political Economy?
A Methodological Forethought

FOREIGN POLICY ANALYSIS*, in its current attempt to grow beyond diplomatic history and fulfill its legitimate aspiration to provide a systematic treatment of the external behaviour of nation states, has already accepted cross disciplinary influences emanating from a wide range of Social Sciences[1] Other than politics and economics. While these influences have, in varying measures, reinforced the intellectual foundation of the subject, they have not been particularly helpful in building up a unified theoretical system. Rather, they have produced a kind of conceptual pluralism, with each single approach imposing its own inherent limitation on the over-all focus of investigation. One possible reason for this lack of coherence seems to be that approaches drawn from other disciplines tend to view the foreign policy role of the state not so much in the context of the mainstream of state activities emanating from historical compulsions-both domestic and external, as in conjunction with specific springboards of motivation from which national action is directed to achieve a number of seemingly unrelated goals in the international sphere.

What seems to have been overlooked, or rather taken for granted, is the view of state as the organized political power which a community employs to achieve aims that are historically relevant and are rooted in the nature of society under consideration. State behaviour, whether in the domestic or in the international context, stems from objective conditions that determine the range and the depth, the expanses as well as the intensity of state activities. The

* Defined here as a study that examines the relevance of external policy of a nation to the goals that it seeks to achieve by influencing the conduct of other nations. It also evaluates the alternative means and ends currently conceivable to anticipate and cope with a generally uncertain future.

state, to be sure, is called upon to play a role that corresponds to the historical development of the national community it happens to represent in the world arena.

This perspective of development is not only important but should be regarded as furnishing the basic premises for any theoretical treatment of the foreign policy of a nation in its totality, as distinguished from its ad hoc manifestations or occasional shifts. The development approach is particularly relevant when one deals with transitional societies of the third world, currently struggling their way through various stages of economic retardation. It sets in bolder relief the contradictions that necessarily arise when nations handicapped by material backwardness seek autonomous ordering of their relations with other enjoying disproportionate prosperity and therefore, a commanding position in the international society.

Within this broad paradigm, foreign policy analysis must look upon the state as a multi-dimensional institution and examine its behaviour as a matter of great complexity, induced as it is by pulls and pushes from many different directions. The state no doubt remains a political institution par excellence but its domain no longer remains confined to politics per se. All along ,and increasingly in our time, the state has been asked to perform a combination of activities that are both within and outside of the political realm. In terms of ends-means relationship, one can think of a schematic set in which political goals tend to be pursued through political as well as nonpolitical means in the same way as nonpolitical goals may be served by political means. The following table would illustrate:

	Example	Ends — Means	*Example*
1	power/security		alliance
		Political — Political	
2	hegemony/influence		foreign aid
		Political — nonpolitical	
3	arms sales	Nonpolitical — political	fomenting subversion/ tension
4	economic survival		economic integration
		Nonpolitical — nonpolitical	

The bove table gives only a simplified illustration of the interwining one notices between the political and the non-political concerns of the state. As a matter of fact, the spill- over of the two in the ends-means spectrum of state activites is so common and often so complete that one cannot but make full allowance for the nonpolitical aspects of foreign relations while trying to assess and explain the external policies of a nation.

Undoubtedly the sheer number of these nonpolitical aspects, apart from their various possible combinations, would baffle any investigation unless one were to pick up and start with the most preponderant of the factors involved. Apart from convenience of analysis, logic would demand that the choice should fall on the basic economic compulsion that defines the path of development for a particular state at a particular time. The reasons are many though the primary one is that nation states in their foreign relations have to operate from and on the strength of the national economy.[2] In fact one of the predominant concerns and perhaps also a principal justification of the modern nation state lies in the management of the national economy. Whether through ownership/ control of the commanding heights of the economy or leverage on its vital sectors, this concern, as we shall see, largely conditions the directions and development of the nation's foreign policy. At the same time, this national economic base is only superficially protected by political boundaries. Increasing interdependence makes it impossible for any national economy today to keep itself insulated from others. The situation today has been admirably summed up in the following words:

> However sacred and inviolable national sovereignty maybe from the political point of view, few national boundaries correspond to economic demarcation lines and few state are self contained economic entities.[3]

Inevitable as it is, when this exposure of the national economy takes place under conditions of inequality, the resultant asymmetry of exchange leads to the phenomenon of dependency which is qualitatively different from the usual dependence noticeable in the "external reliance of well-integrated nation-states on one another."[4] Dependency may be defined as the subjugative incorporation of weaker economic into a global system or subsystem designed to serve the interest of its advanced components. It illustrates how economic relations developed under conditions of actual or potential colonialism tend to continue, albeit in a different form, in the post-colonial era. Such a state of affairs obviously poses a challenge to foreign policy making by a community which finds its political sovereignty largely tied up by economic dependency. An engaging task for the policymakers in these communities naturally consists in the reduction and, as far as practicable, reversal of these economic compulsions so that they could have freer hands in dealing with world issues that affect their interests. Since a majority of the nations states today are confronted with this predicament of diluted sovereignty, economic factors invariably take precedence in the shaping of their foreign policies. Indeed it would be no exaggeration to say that foreign policy for most nations today is primarily dedicated to the immediate cause of economic survival for the ultimate enjoyment of political freedom.

At least for the developing countries, international politics means much more than a mere struggle for power with military security its dominant concern. They attach higher priorities to the goals of national welfare and economic justice. Military security being a chimera for them to pursue in the nuclear age, they construe the questions of security and survival in non military terms which are mostly economic. This means that they have different threat perceptions to cope with, threats that are directed against values such as well-being of the people, political and social autonomy of the nation and, of course, greater justice in international transactions.

II

Given this interdependence of political and economic considerations it is plausible to expect that academic analysis of foreign policy should proceed by harnessing the tools of economic and political science. Unfortunately occasions have been rather few so far when the economists and political scientists have been able to put their heads together. Susan Strange of Chatham House lashes out at this unfortunate segregation of the two disciplines and attributes the tendency to a kind of intellectual apartheid which is fostered as much by arrogance as by diffidence on either side.[5] As a booster to the sagging morale of the political scientist,

Strange has quite ably brought home the point that economics activities do not and cannot take place in a political vacuum.

> Every economic activity only exists in a social frame work of law and custom, in a particular political order and in a particular social structure. If this is true of economic relations between individuals, it is even more true of the economic relations between states. States are never complete strangers to one another, linked only by an economic bargain as individuals may sometimes be (if rarely). States are sufficiently few in numbers and sufficiently long-lasting that behind each economic bargain struck with another state there lies a complex web of historical association, political and strategic conflict or cooperation and social and cultural sympathy and antipathy.[6]

To be fair enough, mention may be made of a couple of earlier efforts to coordinate the politics and economics of foreign policy in spite of the alleged segregation of the two disciplines. In one of these works jointly sponsored by the Woodrow Wilson Foundation and National Planning forum of the USA[7], the starting assumption for a political economy approach to American foreign policy is that economic policymakers have to work under limitations imposed by historical and political conditions, which is why economic policy alone cannot achieve much in the field of foreign policy. The other one worth mentioning is by James R Schlesinger[8] who also recognizes the limitations of a purely economic approach to foreign policy analysis and points out:

> Economic analysis transmutes itself into political economy when certain goals or social values are widely accepted as given that there can be a narrowing of the range of choise.

In other words , once goals have been fixed by the political process, it would be convenient to use economics to suggest the most effective allocation of resources for their realization. However, this view of politics as a constraint on economics has nothing flattering about it. While it barely conceals the injured vanity of the economist that he could do things better if only left alone, the fact is that in the complex society of today no one — the politicians or the administrator, the trade unionist or the businessmen, would let the others alone and have it their way. Consequently it is not merely economics but politics too which is equally circumscribed. This is partly attributed to what may be called the dwindling autonomy of political decisions. The fact that the State sets before itself certain objectives and may choose political or non political means to achieve those ends is not sufficient to help us understand the genesis of the choice and the rationale involved in it. Rather it should be important to ask why certain lines of action, political or nonpolitical, are chosen in preference to others as the best way to accomplish the given objectives. The fact is that there is an unmistakable relationship between the different segments of public affairs. Decisions of the state do not fall neatly into political or economic baskets, though conceptually it is possible to separate the one from the other. Such notional dissociation may be helpful for limited purposes and relevant only up to a certain level of abstraction beyond which one must fall back on the interdisciplinary line of enquiry. From this viewpoint, Political Economy should, hopefully, supply the missing focus of interdependence.

At this point, a word of caution will be called for lest political economy, as it has grown as a branch of non positivist economics, should be found wanting for the purpose of foreign policy analysis. It will be important to recognize that for the most part, Political Economy is not a synthesis or intermingling of Economic and the Political Sciences but only an extension of normative economics to make good for the shortcomings of positive economics. It is economics tempered by the value judgments that are socially determined. Thus in the vocabulary of a leading economist in the field.

Political Economy.... is not scientific economics, a collections of value free generalizations about the way in which economic systems work. It is a discussion of principles of public policy **in the economic field** and while it makes appeal to the findings of the economics science, it also involves assumptions which in the nature of things lie outside positive science and which are essentially **normative** in character.[9]

The above definition contains two qualifications which should be considered crucial to the kind of foreign policy analysis we have in mind. In the first place, it indicates the inadequacy of value-free, positive economics and makes us aware of the pitfalls we ought to avoid while applying conventional economic formulations to the study of foreign relations of nations. Thus the central conceptual frame of any economic analysis, viz. the existence of an inexorable market mechanism needs to be substantially modified because the international system, though basically structured for competitive self-promotion of its units, is itself subject to various forms of manipulation through shifting allegiance and campaign for new found values (other than brutal self interest) among the units concerned. Besides the very rationale of benefit maximization through marginal preferences would have to labour under a good deal of equivocation in international politics because the preferences structure of nations remains largely indeterminate and benefits are usually related to costs ,through rarely overmatched ,by the means of wise, if not wild, guesswork. In contrast to the economists, concern for efficient allocation of scarce resources, international politics need not always admit of such a thing as "dearer butter, therefore more margarine", because the limits of public commitment here are governed not so much by the possibility of substitution as by the necessity of accomplishing goals which have socially determined priorities.

More importantly, rational and autonomous choice of alternatives is not easy to obtain in international politics. The overriding elements of coercion and intimidation that are available in inordinate proportions to some actors largely destroy free choice for others. It is this predicament of restricted choice that constitutes the principal concern of the weaker members of the international society, who therefore have to devise some special strategies for enhancing national economic capability and frame their foreign policies accordingly. Within this framework, fixation of goals, allocation of priorities and choice of instruments in both economic and political spheres of State activity will have to be directed to the achievement of autonomy.

It is precisely here that the second important qualification in Robbins's definition viz. the question of normative decision-making arises. This involves identification of those vital assumption that ought to guide normative decision-making. For these assumptions to be valid and meaningful ,they must have close link with the objective social necessities which have overriding importance for the community in question. Incidentally ,to look for the relevant social basis of public policy one has to take a different view of economics as a wider and more fundamental social process and politics as its sustaining condition. As Engels[10] wrote:

> Political economy in the modest sense is the science of laws governing the production and exchange of the **material means** of subsistence in the economy and is concerned with the study of social relations of production and distribution in their development.

One can take this point a little farther and apply it on the international plane. Just as in the development of societies there is a significant correspondence between the forces of production and the production relations they create, similarly in the relations of nations involving exposure of one economy to the other, there would arise relations of compatibility as well as conflict, depending on the nature of production relations each nation would symbolize for the others.

III

This line of thinking seems to indicate some light at the tunnel's end for our present quest for a proper methodology that would assist general theoretical treatment of the foreign policy of nations **undergoing or on the threshold**[11] of social transformation. It suggests quite a few significant steps that would lead to any meaningful generalization.

First, one has to look for some broad perception — or lack of it — on the part of the national decision making authority regarding the extent of contradiction between existing material dependence and the claim of autonomous policymaking in the external sphere.

Second , note should be taken of the manner in which the aforesaid contradiction does or does not get exacerbated when national policymakers seek to handle the issue of dependence through international diplomacy. The point to be investigated is how far the policymaker can allow external economic inputs to flow into the national economy(a) without jeopardizing its viability and (b) without over exposing the economy to the risks of external manipulations.

Third , it will be necessary to examine the kind of counter-jeopardy tactics a nation should adopt when it happens to be on the brink of a critical overexposure. Technically these may be called the tactics of 'dependency reversal' which are likely to set in motion a twofold tendency toward self-restoration of the economy, namely, (a) the inward –looking tendency expressing itself in a renewed pledge for self-reliance and(b) the outward-looking tendency requiring a restructuring of complementarity with select economies abroad. Each tendency in its turn would generate a different kind of foreign policy orientation and one has to see how far each, in the long run, would be consistent with the stated objective of national autonomy in the matter of policymaking.

This finally, leads to an evaluative phase which will identify some important indicators on the basis of which one could argue if in the management of the national economy and foreign relations the decision-making authorities have or have not been able to contribute to an improved ability of the nation to order its relations with others, consistent with its inherent dignity and legitimate aspirations.

In the chapters that follow an attempt will be made to apply this line of enquiry to the evolving foreign policy of India which provides by far the most instructive instance of the innovative efforts of a nation to work out a foreign policy that has clear organic connections with a none too modest ambition of economic self-promotion. For a country like India, foreign policymaking has been essentially an art of making both ends meet, the economic and the political. More important ,the latter of these ends cannot flourish freely as long as the former remains retarded. In fact one cannot help noticing an unresolved contradiction between the kind of external role India aspires for and the economic constraints she must overcome at home. And the contradiction is hardly attenuated by the fact that a continuing power asymmetry in the world arena has all along denied India political stronghold commensurate with the prominence she desires. To give credibility to her external aspirations she has to do two things at the same time: a pragmatic ordering of her objectives in world politics and a resolute cultivation of the social base which would provide the necessary support structure for a meaningful pursuit of these objectives. Hence, one of the major preoccupations of foreign policymaking in India consists in striking a balance between the recourse of diplomacy and those of domestic development, the objective being not to allow the commitments in either sector to work at cross purposes. The methods that have been tried in this experiment, the hazards that have been encountered on the way and the social adjustments that have occurred in the process- constitute the core of the present enquiry into the political economy of India's foreign policy.

References

1. Prominent among these are Social Psychology, Management, Strategic studies, Political Anthropology and the Communications Sciences. For relevant literature see Richard L Cottam, *Foreign Policy Motivations* University of Pittsburgh press 1977; Richard L Merritt *Communication in International* politics, University of Illinois Press Urbana 1972; Richard C. Snyder,(ed) *Foreign Policy Decision Making* Free Press New York , 1962; Norman Jacobs (ed) *Making Foreign Policy in a Nuclear Age*, Foreign Policy Association New York,1965; J. M. Reinhardt *Foreign Policy and National Integration*, Yale University, South East Asian Studies, New Haven,1971.
2. cf. Professor Modelski's concept of Power Input in *A Theory of Foreign Policy*, pp 23-28 Center of International Studies Princeton University, Praeger, New York, 1962
3. United Nations Publication No ST/ECA/190, *Multinational Corporations in World Development*, p 3, New York, 1973
4. James A. Caporaso Dependence and Dependency in the Global System, *International Organization*, volume 32, No 1, p 13, winter issue 1978
5. Susan Strange *International Economic Relations: the Need for on Interdisciplinary Approach*, in Roger Morgan (ed) *The study of International Affairs: Essays in Kenneth Younger*, p 63. RIIA, OUP, London, 1972.
6. ibid, pp 65-66
7. William Y. Elliott (ed), *The Political Economy of American Foreign Policy; its Concepts, Strategies and Limits*, Henry Holt, New York. 1955
8. James R. Schlesinger, *The Political Economy of National Security*, p 23, Praeger, New York, 1980
9. Lionel Charles Robbins, *Political Economy: Past and Present*, pp 2-3, Columbia University Press New York, 1976 (emphasis added).
10. cit. *Political Economy in the Soviet Union : Some Problems of Teaching the Subject* (translated from Pod Znamenem Markiszma July-Aug 1943)
11. These expressions only indicate the broad range of national societies which best fit in with the developmental approach to foreign policy analysis. While they admit of variations in the specific constraints and advantages for each individual nation, they emphasize the problems and prospects facing all of them.

2

A Dependent Economy's Quest for Independent Foreign Policy

ONE THING that India did not lack at the hour of independence was a foreign policy outlook, broadly delineating what the country deemed necessary for achieving a batter international environment. What 'however, remained to be spelled out was how the new nation expected to promote its own immediate and long-term interests until such time as it would not be possible to bring about the desired systemic change. Insofar as a pronounced idealist-reformist attitude to world affairs characterized the pre-independence thinking of the national leaders, it was reassuring to hear Jawaharlal Nehru the Prime Minister who also took charge of foreign affairs, say in the course of an early full-scale parliamentary debate on foreign policy; [1]

> Whatever policy we may lay down the art of conducting the foreign affairs of a country lies in finding out what is most advantageous to country. We may talk about international goodwill and mean what we say. We may talk about peace and freedom and earnestly mean what we say. But in the ultimate analysis, a government functions for the good of the country it governs and no government dare do anything which in the short or long run is manifestly to the disadvantage of that country.

So far as India was concerned, the components of what counted toward 'the good of the country' from its own standpoint were however left unspecified — probably to be worked out as time rolled on and understandably not to be emphasized in haste lest that should cloud the more enlightened, other-regarding vision of world affairs which had become a faith with the nationalist movement.[2] Hence most of the commitments of the pre independence era found their way to the agenda of post-independence foreign policy making. Ideals such as those of world peace and disarmament, abolition of colonialism and racial discrimination, promotion of equality of nation, ascendancy of morality over power politics and economic emancipation of all backward areas of the world-were all faithfully incorporated and frequently reaffirmed as the stated goals of India's foreign policy.

I. Policy Outlook and External Support Base

From the very beginning, therefore, there were two sets of policy objectives for which India would be working in world affairs- the unspecified self-regarding interests as perceived from time and the much publicized other regarding concerns as traditionally defined by the ruling elite of country. The relative weight to be assigned to each set and the components thereof was thus going to be a function of two factors; capability at the command of the new political order and its varying perception of the urgency of each objective in relation to others.

Tall as these objectives were, their pursuit required the attainment of a sufficiently significant international status which alone give the new nation necessary leverage and credibility with others. Insofar as some of these objectives, while aimed at reforming the international system, also posed a challenge to its erstwhile beneficiaries, a situation of potential confrontation may be said to have been implicit in the otherwise peaceful formulation of the country's foreign policy. This is turn was likely to impose greater burden on the limited diplomatic resources of the country. Of course, nothing was ever planned to be done unilaterally, but rallying of forces was not immediately forthcoming and would itself take some shrewd investment of whatever diplomatic resources were available at the moment. In any case ,there was no denying the fact that the global tasks conceived for India's foreign policy were simply out of proportion to the capability then at the command of the nation.[3]

Aware of this limitation, the Indian leaders adopted two tactical lines — one intended to gloss over the country's lack of effective international power and the other to work for the achievement of an international status the potential for which to be sure ,was not lacking. The first was reflected in the habitual rhetoric of the Indian statesman about the constraints, dangers and futility of power understood in the conventional sense of coercive capability. Prime Minister Nehru made it a point to preach to the outside world the wisdom of eschewing power politics "the very process of which precipitates the conflict which it has sought to avoid,"[4] and also to chide his critics at home who believed "the possession of great armed might 'or great financial power' should necessarily lead to right decisions or a right mental outlook."[5]

The second tactial line was less naïve and clearly, had great innovative value. It was directed to the creation of an international subsystem which would give India a vantage position from which to pressure the entrenched interests of the larger system into an arrangement of mutual give-and-take. This was precisely the diplomatic utility that was ultimately derived from non-alignment, though admittedly, it did not present itself in this cut-and-dried form when non-alignment was first contemplated by the Indian statesmen. Of course, there is a lot of official disclaimer to the effect that the policy of non-alignment was never conceived in the spirit of building up a "third force".[6]

There is also the weighty opinion[7] that non-alignment was some sort of a spontaneous, as distinguished from calculated, response to the bipolar division of the world, though inherently it was a "logical extension of the conflict between....nationalism and military blocs." Mainly ,it was proposed "to keep away from the power politics of groups, aligned against one another" so that the nation could take part in international politics with its "own policy and not merely as a satellite of another nation."[8] Ideologically too, a national preference for equidistance might have been influential in the adoption of the non-aligned attitude.

But these explanations mostly in the nature of rationalizing a policy stance which was supposed only to highlight the sovereignty of decision –making and which needed to be assiduously protected from any insinuations of alliance building, did not and could not wish away the fundamental lack of capability which India must make good either on the domestic front or in the international sphere, preferably both, if there was to be a serious pursuit of the country's national interests, enlightened or otherwise.

It was not so much the concept of non-alignment as the worldwide movement it sparked off which may be said to have provided India with the most useful external base from which to operate in the world politics. And it would be mincing matters to suppose that the balancing role of an expanding third area, dealing with but not committed to any of the rival power groups, should have escaped the searching eyes of the Indian policymakers who really believed that India being no" odd little nation somewhere" ought to count "more and more" in world affairs[9]. On one occasion, Nehru himself was inclined to call it a "third Area "(instead of "Third bloc") which "does not want war, works for peace in a positive way and believes in cooperation."[10] In due course this Third Area was destined to develop into an international subsystem having constant and in many ways effective interaction with the larger system. Insofar as India happens to be the founder member of the non-aligned group and remains in the forefront of the non-aligned movement, it will be useful to have in reserve an external base for the nation to operate in world politics. It not only precluded foreign policy thinking from an exclusively egocentric deliberations and concerted action. After all, in these days of congregative diplomacy , the importance of the widest possible articulation and aggregation of interests cannot be exaggerated. What arose, therefore, as one nation's answer to the problem of bloc rivalry in the postwar world, ultimately expanded into the common concern of most new nations joining the world community during the last three decades. In fact rare was the case when a people having attained statehood during this period decided against joining the non-alignment movement[11] —a fact which is a tribute to the farsightedness of the Indian statesmen who originated it.[12]

From India's standpoint, her consistent diplomatic interest in the whole process is not merely justified by the need to preserve the leadership status that has devolved upon her. It should also be looked upon as a worthwhile investment in building up a much needed support base for her policy beyond her territorial boundary. To the extent Indian authorities want to adopt an international posture free from the overpowering tatics of the giant states, they can derive added strength from a programme of cooperation with like-minded nations who, by their sheer number, compel global attention.

II. The Question of External Economic Linkage

Autonomy of foreign policy, however, does not thrive simply on the numerical support available abroad, though that should be regarded as a very necessary condition for its successful implementation. The ultimate and, perhaps, the perennial basis for the autonomy part of it clearly consists in the ability of national leadership to harness and utilize internal power inputs[13] generated and multiplied through a consistent programme for the material uplift of the nation. In this respect the nations adhering to the non-aligned outlook of foreign policy seem to share a common experience. The kind of extended nationalism which creates the superstructure of a non –aligned world subsystem and establishes a feedback relationship with it is itself tied to a larger sustaining structure. This relates to the growth process of the national economies as determined by their interaction with the world economy. For the most part, the national economics of the newly liberated countries were in pretty bad shape after years of colonial exploitation and in dire need not only of thorough restructuring but carful political management in order to fend off the debilitating effects of the uneven yet unavoidable transactions with advanced industrial economics. This means that foreign policy for these countries will not only have to be synchronized with the demands of economic growth but may itself have to be a catalytic agent to ensure the right kind of interaction of the national with the world economy.

Coupled with aggregative international action, therefore, a programme of national economic management constitutes the most significant independent variable which will largely govern the drift of a country's foreign policy toward assured autonomy or renewed subservience. In the case of India , the national leadership was keenly aware of the interdependence of economic and foreign policy. Comparable to the 'national interest' allusion in Nehru's statement cited earlier , another rare theme in his speeches, rare because of its unalloyed pragmatism, deserves to be quoted *in extenso*:

> Ultimately, foreign policy is the outcome of economic policy, and until India has properly evolved her economic policy, her foreign policy will be rather vague, rather inchoate and rather groping. It is well for us to

> say that we stand for peace and freedom and yet that does not convey much to anybody, except a pious hope...what then do we stand for? Well, you have to develop this argument in the economic field. As it happens today, in spite of the fact that we have been for sometime in authority as a government I regret that we have not produced any constructive economic schemes or economic policy so far.... Nevertheless we shall have to do so and when we do so, **that will govern our foreign policy** more than all the speeches in this House.[14]

Tardiness in a vital matter like formulation of national economic policy was too unusual to be explained in terms of the excuses that were immediately available, such as the pressing circumstances of partition, communal disturbance, tension over Kashmir or preoccupation with constitution-making. The real reason ,however , seems to be the general ambivalence which gripped the new government when a final break had to be made with the country's colonial past. Decisive action was needed to cut loose the manifold strings of economic bondage which remained intact even after transfer of political power. Of the numerous instances of this bondage two were most glaring, viz, the imperial preference system and the sterling area operation to which India was linked by the Ottawa Agreement (1932). Opposition of Indian National Congress to the impairing effects of these arrangement on India's fiscal autonomy was only recent memory. Overwhelming resentment has also been voiced forth by the Indian business community. The Federation of Indian Chambers of Commerce and Industry pointed out:[15]

> It is a matter of common knowledge that as a result of this agreement... trade has been diverted from India's best customers into one channel alone.

In addition there was the wide and deep penetration of British and other foreign investments into the economy, discussed more fully in a later chapter.[16] These and similar matters raised a fundamental issue for the new rulers of India: whether and how far it was feasible to extricate economic linkage left over by the previous colonial regime. The options open to them were either a radical breach calling for a completely new set of economic relationship or a continuation of the *status quo* in the hope of successful management of economic dependency by dint of the new found political powers. Eventually it was the latter line of least resistance and gradual change that was found expedient. The new government did not denounce the 1939 Indo-British trade agreement; nor did it press for a new agreement. On the contrary, it engaged in transforming the old relationship as part of its wider programme of establishing 'friendship with every nation' It took little time to overcome the psychological hangover of all pre-independence animosities against the machination of imperialism and brush aside all constitutional-political objections raised by a sizeable section of parliamentarians against the proposed induction of the Republic into an association headed by the British monarch. Even before independence was actually proclaimed, Nehru had no qualms about pleading for Commonwealth membership, In his words,[17]

> For a long time past we have taken a pledge on Independence Day that India must sever her connection with Great Britain because that connection has become an emblem of British domination .... But what I would like this House to consider is this: when these words and these *labels* are fast changing their meaning and in the world there is no isolation, you cannot live apart form the others. You must cooperate or you must fight.

This is not the place to attempt a critique of the argument advanced by Nehru in defence of his revised opinion about British imperialism which twenty years back he had called "the most objectionable and aggressive manifestation of a world phenomenon...called capitalism"[18] nor will it be relevant to reiterate the various personal as well as political considerations which influenced his decisions and infuriated public opinion, especially of the leftist hue.[19] The point that needs to be explored here is the immediate and/or long-term view of national interests to which Nehru did not relate his Commonwealth decision. Besides, since it symbolized an accommodative approach not merely to wards Britain but towards the whole of the capitalist world as such it would be interesting to see if and how an open-ended approach like this could be consistent with the fundamental condition of conducting foreign relations in real national interest, viz. the autonomy of decision.

So far as immediate national interests were concerned, it has been pointed out by a noted India-analyst who has devoted a good deal of expertise in understanding Nehru's political mind[20] that "by far the most important (consideration) was the realization that India could not remain isolated in a world of great tension — the cold war was then a harsh reality —and that the commonwealth link was the most advantageous" This line of thinking seems to attach undue importance to the cold war syndrome to which the Indian reaction has been consistently one of avoiding all unnecessary entanglements and against which in any case British association had little to promise as a protective shelter from the possible fall-out of the cold war. Similarly, using the commonwealth as a possible platform "to render greater assistance to the substantial communities of Indian settlers in south Africa, Malaya, British Guiana, and other parts of the Empire" would no more than marginally affect the situation unless there was some substantial prospect of a bilateral settlement of the issue of Indian minorities abroad. Brecher also draws one's attention to some compelling economic considerations as follows:

> The bulk of India's trade was with the commonwealth; its foreign exchange resources were tied up in the sterling area; its armed forces depended on British-made weapons.

In short the argument is one of perpetuating the existing relation of dependence which is however' the last thing one contemplates when an independent posture in foreign relations seems to be at stake. Applied to a wider field of external association the same argument takes the following form in the writing of a senior Indian official who has played a prominent role in the economic diplomacy of the country:

> When Nehru surveyed the scene in 1947, what did he find? India needed new markets besides the old ones; she needed new technology in addition to what had been imported to enable the British to fight the war; she needed new sources of capital besides the sterling balances. Hence the policy to forge new links and to transform not destroy old ones. It was called a policy of non-alignment which meant in fact, a policy of being aligned to every nation of the world in friendship on a basis of equality and for mutual benefit.[21]

In other words, the basic structural deficiencies of the Indian economy and the need to repair them with external input form whatever source they were available was going to be the rationale of India's International economic relations for several years to come. Whereas in the case of the commonwealth it was governed by the temporary expedient of economic linkage with the retiring colonial power,[22] it was reinforced by a general urge to make India a beneficiary of global economic process. Since Nehru himself set this long term pattern, it will be relevant to recall how he thought this was going to provide an even greater motivation to India's diplomacy then the conventional view of non-alignment:[23]

> When I say that we should not align ourselves with any power blocs, obviously it does not mean that we should not be closer in our relations with some countries than with other. That depends on entirely different factors, chiefly economic, political, agricultural and many other factors... While remaining quite apart from power blocs... our relation can become as close as possible in the economic or other domain with such countries with whom we can easily develop them

A great measure of flexibility was thus implicit in the general doctrine of non-alignment where it concerned the economic interests of the nation. India's economic diplomacy with other nations was thus neatly cured of any ideological or political preferences and was directed to the exploration and cultivation of all accessible areas of economic cooperation. The logic went more or less along the following line: the more broad-based and diversified the linkage, the greater was the possibility of reducing the dependence on one particular sector.[24] Given the non –permanence of friendship or enmity in diplomacy, this approach, though prone to accusations of opportunism, is likely to contribute to national interests as long as the existing and evolving linkages are primarily related to the strengthening of the domestic base of power inputs. Since there is no convincing evidence to doubt the intention of the Nehru Government "to make India economically strong and militarily.....as strong as we can," it would be reasonable to assume that his initial decision not to sever connections with the Western capitalist states, when matched by the development of new connections elsewhere, would lead to a wide margin of maneuver, so that ,in his words," one need not put all one's eggs in one basket" or seek" help at the cost of one's self respect".[25] In fact replying to the charge that government "incline(d) more towards the Anglo-American bloc" as evidenced by greater "economic and other bonds with U.K and U.S.A than with other countries" in the early fifties, Nehru admitted:

> That is a situation we have inherited and unless we develop new bonds we shall have to continue as we are doing... I cannot deny that there is danger and risk when a country begins to depend upon another. Whatever the form it takes dependence is always bad, one should be on one's guard against it. Yet a country placed as India is today, has inevitably to depend on other countries for certain essential things. We are not industrialized enough to produce all that we need. We have to depend on other countries for most of the things for our Army or Air force or our Navy requires. Of course ,we must try to build up basic industries so that we can produce things our essential needs...In the meanwhile we have got to get them from somewhere.... It is very difficult for us to build new channels of trade and commerce overnight. We are perfectly prepared to explore these possibilities; for instance, we are perfectly prepared to deal with the Soviet Union or any other country that can supply us with the particular goods we need.[26]

The above statement, significantly, was made within a year of the launching of the First Five Year Plan of the country for which foreign assistance flow was estimated at Rs 156 crores —a bare 10% of the draft plan outlay of Rs 1493 crores,[27] most of which was to come from the Anglo-American sources. Foreign trade figures continued to show a similar inclination with import from the sterling area countries varying between 51.1% and 52.3% up to 1954-55 and import from the dollar area ranging from 29.3% to 16.7% for the same period. Total capital inflow from U.K. and U.S.A at the end of 1955was respectively of the order of Rupees 390.72 crores and Rupees 39.76 crores out of a total of Rs. 469.91 crores[28] In fact the desired diversification of external economic relations was nowhere near sight until the signing of the first Indo-Soviet Trade Agreement (December 2,1953) and subsequent Soviet interest in India's industrial development. Nonetheless, it is worth noting that even during its formative years independent India's foreign policy showed some appreciable advanced thinking about the way economic compulsions were going to determine the contours of that policy. Indeed ,it marked the beginning of an experiment for which there was practically no precedent in recorded diplomacy. To cling to the ideal of autonomous policymaking while a whole array of economic constraints worked in opposite direction and at the same time to expect external economic cooperation without being drawn into the on-going power struggle was clearly ahead of the existing theories and practice of foreign policy. What the Indian experiment involved was, therefore , a slow evolution of a new theory, maturing through trial and error that would give it the necessary refinement for a more confident application in the years to come.

III. Theoretical Bases of Policy Operation

To sum up, the theoretical basis of India's foreign policy seems to rest primarily on the interaction of three main variables:

(a) The compulsions of national reconstruction;
(b) The complementarities to be achieved with other stronger national economies ; and
(c) The consolidation of an international subsystem under the banner of non –alignment.

These variables ,severally and collectively, would shape the specifics of national interest that come under the generic value of autonomy in external affairs. It would be incumbent upon the policymaker to anticipate and, as far as possible ,regulate the interaction of these variables so that maximum value is gained at the least payable cost. Some sort of a cost –benefit analysis would, therefore, be implicit in the operation of foreign policy though 'cost' and 'benefit' in this context have a complex connotation. They have to be constructed as a mix of political, social and economic consequences that are supposed to flow from the interaction of one variable upon another. For instance, when economic development is given primacy for some social reason or other, it could hold out not one but a variety of complementarities to be achieved with other economies. An attempted complementarity, however ,need not always be neutral in its effect upon the larger value premise of autonomy which subsume all specific national interests.

Whenever a certain pattern of complementarity would seem to run counter to the basic value premise, policy makers will clearly need to have a second look at the strategies of economic development e.g. structural changes reflected by the volume and pattern of capital investment and if these appear sound enough ,urgency would arise for a rearrangement of the complementarities in question. This in turn, would set special tasks for diplomacy to explore new areas of economic linkage in addition to or a substitute for the existing ones. Normally, this will be the order in which the variables of 'development' and 'complementarity' are likely to be managed by the national decision-makers; for after all the very choice of development strategies itself has to be an exercise in autonomous decision-making. Consequently, if it appears, when activating a familiar source of external input for domestic development, that the supply of input would be conditional upon a revision of the development strategy, complementarity in such a case would naturally be looked upon as a costly venture impinging upon the generic value of autonomy. Conditional complementarity may also affect other apparently unrelated zones of decision-making, for example, attitude and action towards domestic or international political order. In either case foreign policy would generally follow the course of political economy and give vent to the basic concern for defending independence of national decision-making. To the extent foreign policy would fail to register this concern, it would reflect an actual or impending symptom of sovereignty being at bay.

The variable of complementarity, however may itself take precedence under certain special circumstances over the variable of economic growth. For instance, if the decision-making have or develop ideological predilection in favour of a particular social order, then there will be an irresistible tendency to move along a given path of complementarity such as one notices in the case of economic integration of the EEC and CMEA countries. Since the ideological position of national decision makers cannot be radically different from what existing production relations within the country would generally warrant, it will be necessary to keep track of the structure of production relations underlying the country's political economy. When this subnational dimension enters into the theory of foreign policy, the question of choice and management of complementarities would lose much of its weight. To the extent change of the internal economic order as distinguished from the simple issue of prosperity getting better of backwardness, constitutes the dominant ideological concern of economic development, foreign policy is bound to develop a specific area orientation that is linked with the external complementarities demanded by social change at home rather than switch form one area to another to suit temporary economic expediency or occasional political ambitions.

This brings us to the consideration of third important variable of non-alignment as an international subsystem With its undeniable promise of a much needed support base for the international postures of the Indian authorities it goes without saying that the considerations of economic reconstruction and complementarities cannot be and, perhaps, should not be spelled out without a direct reference to their relevance to the non-aligned subsystem. In this respect, a penetrating observation of the celebrated Swedish economist Gunnar Myrdal merits serious attention:

> The underdeveloped countries have joined their forces in making demands upon the rest of the world in the course of general encounters in the various organs of their readiness for actual economic cooperation among themselves, which is put to the test in relations between neighboring countries in the regional organizations is feeble or non-existent. Not only the former colonies, but also the other underdeveloped countries, demonstrate a **psychological and political fixation** in relation to one or several "metropolitan" countries-to which they react positively or negatively, and their economic relations tend to be under the same spell. [29]

The nexus of political connection which India has been able to develop with a large number of developing countries under the banner of non-alignment could very well present her with an opportunity to attempt a common campaign against this "metropolitan fixation" and would certainly do so as the cold war syndrome which provided original rationale of non-alignment tends to give way to a gradual normalisation of international relations. In fact as economic development proceeds in these countries under diverse circumstances, each country starting at a different point of time and with a different set of resource endowments, it is highly likely that sooner or later these countries would stumble upon the great differential of comparative advantage that each has been able to create in relation to the rest, so that economic stratification within the non-aligned subsystem may itself lead to a search on their part for intra-subsystem complementarities. So far as India is concerned, such a development will not only be welcome but absolutely necessary in case her experiment with open-ended friendship with every nation without giving away the supreme value of national independence remains unfinished or, at the worst, proves unworkable because of the inherent contradiction of such a goal with the hegemonistic tendencies of the major economies of the world. In such an event "interdeveloping" with the less developed countries would probably be the best alternative to follow to make for the substance rather than the semblance of an independent foreign policy

References

1. Speech in the Constituent Assaembly, December 4, 1947, rep. Jawaharlal Nerhru, *India's Foreign Policy: Selected Speeches*, p28, Government of India, Publications Division, New Delhi, 1961.
2. By far the best account of early expression of Indian Foreign Policy is to be found in Bimla Prasad, *The Origins of Indian Foreign Policy;: The Indian National Congress and World Affairs* Bookland, Calcutta, 1962
3. As Nehru admitted in the *Lok Sabha* on March 8, 1948: "We are not frankly speaking influential enough to affect international event very much"
4. Address at Columbia University, October 17,1949, *Jawaharlal Nehru: Visit to America*, p 30, John, New York, 1950.
5. Reply to foreign affairs debate in Lok Sabha, December 9, 1958, Nehru *India's Foreign Policy, op. cit.* p80
6. Foreign affairs debate, December 17, 1957, ibid. 77-79.
7. Michael Brecher, *India and World Politics: Krishna Menon's View of the World* , pp3-4, O.U.P., London, 1968
8. Broadcast from New Delhi, September 7. 1946, Nehru, *op.cit.* p2.
9. A recurrent theme in most of the foreign policy speeches of Nehru.
10. *Jawaharlal Nehru's speeches,* vol II p 326, GOI Publications Division, New Delhi.
11. The movement which has now 86 full members, 10 potential ones and 12 observer organizations encompasses over half of the globe. *MEA Report*, pp 76-77
12. In a prophetic utterance on December 4 1947 Nehru said : "I have no doubt that fairly soon, in the course of two or three years, the world will find this attitude (of nonalignment) justified and that India will not only be respected by the major protagonists in the struggle for power, but a large number of smaller nations which today are rather helpless will probably look to India more than to other countries for a lead in such matters," *Foreign Policy*, p27
13. An expression which finds excellent exposition in Modelski, *op.cit.*

14. Nehru, *Foreign Policy, op.cit,* pp 24-25 (emphasis added)
15. FICCI, *Correspondence and Relevant Documents* 1936, vol 111 p 18 Proceedings of the 9th Annual Meeting, Delhi, April 1936.
16. see Chapter IV *infra*
17. *Constituent Assembly Debates* (22 January 1947), vol II ,P 321,GOI Press, Faridabad, reprint 1966.
18. Address at Poona Youth Conference, December 1928, J.S. Bright (ed) *Nehru: Before and after Independence,* p 56, New Delhi (updated)
19. See Nicholas Mansergh, *Documents and Speeches of British Commonwealth Affairs,* vol II pp 847-857, RIIA, London,1953; *Peoples Age,* Bombay, March 21,1948 and *New Times,* Moscow, January 12, 1948
20. Michael Brecher, *Nehru: A Political Biography,* pp 417-418, OUP, London,1959
21. K.B Lall, *Nehru and International Economic Cooperation,* in B.R. Nanda(ed) *Indian Foreign Policy: Nehru Years,* p187, Vikas, New Delhi,1976
22. Whereas the formal decision to stay within the Commonwealth is generally believed to have been an 'act of free will' on the part of India, there is also no gainsaying the fact that the British government was equally anxious to keep India within its sphere of influence. See the significant reference in the correspondence of the Cabinet Mission concerning (i) a proposed treaty "to provide...for a matter of common defence interest and for all necessary matters arising out of the transfer of power" such as "British strategic interests and right of European British subjects in India" and (ii) the need to be discreet about not clarifying if independence did not mean "independence outside the British commonwealth." See also Prime Minister Attlee's views on the matter in Cyriac Maprayil, *Nehru and the Commonwealth,* Radiant Publishers, New Delhi,1976.
23. Speech delivered at ICWA, New Delhi, March 22,1949,Nehru, *Foreign Policy, op. cit.* p 47
24. J. Bandopadhyay, The Economic Bases of Foreign Policy, *India Quarterly* vol xxv, pp 359-373, New Delhi 1969
25. *CAD,* March,1948, *Nehru Speeches* 1946-49,pp21-219 GOI Publications Division, New Delhi 1949.
26. Reply to foreign affairs debates, Lok Sabha, June 12, 1952,Nehru, *Foreign Policy, op cit.* p59
27. Subsequently both these figures went up, total foreign assistance utilised during the First Plan being Rs 204 crores, i.e 9.8% of the total outlay of Rs 2069 crores.
28. *RBI* Bulletin, September,1958.
29. Gunner Myrdal, *An International Economy: Problems and Prospects,* p7, Harper Torchbook edn, Harper & Row, New York, 1969.

3

A Developing Economy's Handling of External Aid

THE RULING ELITE OF INDIA, despite the strong conservative undercurrents to which they occasionally adjust their social outlook,[1] have generally regarded the State as an active agent of economic growth, with centrally coordinated plans providing the necessary sense of direction. As the role of the state gets heightened in the process, its activities inevitably impinge on the same, limited reservoir of resources which also feed private enterprise in the country. In resolving the problems of resources mobilisation which crops up when domestic supply of investible resources remains inelastic, the State has necessarily to look for additional sources of development inputs if it wants private enterprise to thrive at the same time. The problem is further aggravated by the fact that India's foreign trade being what it was for several decades, it was well nigh impossible for the authorities to think of financing the enhanced import requirements of a developing economy entirely by export earning.[2] Consequently, recourse to external inputs for economic development was felt unavoidable. To the extent this aid dependence become a persistent feature of the economy bringing in its wake new vulnerability to external economic and political manipulation, the handling of foreign aid continued to be a standing concern of the country's foreign policy.

An attempt will be made in the following sections to examine how foreign policy of India acted as the handmaid of the country's political economy in dealing with the dangers of excessive aid dependence.

I. Aid as Dependence

In its early phase, public thinking on economic plans in India recognized the need for supplementary foreign assistance to be received in manageable and not in menacing proportions. The Advisory Planning Board, official precursor of the Planning Commission, suggested in its report published in January 1947:

> It is clear that a very large proportion of the funds required for development purposes will have to be raised by internal borrowing; but the possibility of external borrowing should also be kept in mind so far as this is compatible with the preservation of national economic freedom.....In the immediate future a very large amount of capital equipment will have to be obtained from abroad as we can exercise little or no influence over the rate at which it become available. We are necessarily dependent on this. We believe, however, that as a potential purchaser India is relatively well placed for it seems likely that we shall have no difficulty in providing foreign exchange to pay for this capital equipment either in the ordinary course of trade or by use of our sterling assets or by external borrowing.[3]

It was understood from the very beginning that a steady flow of foreign capital equipments was essential to economic planning . Consequently it should be incumbent upon the country's economic diplomacy to influence, as far as possible, the rate of the flow. At the same time existing reserves of foreign exchange and their replenishment through international trade were supposed to meet the debt obligations arising out of foreign assistance.

A simple strategy like this could and should work as long as the size of the development plan and especially its foreign exchange components are kept within manageable limit. That is why the first five year plan which utilised foreign aid of a very modest order (Rs 189 crores i.e. 9.6% of actual public sector outlay of Rs 1960 crores) and also could draw on the accumulated sterling balances with U.K. as well as a not too bad trade turn-over, did not encounter any rough weather. On the international plane too, the coming into being of the IMF, IBRD (1946) and the Colombo Plan (January 1950) has raised new hopes of obtaining external assistance through multilateral channels.

Against this background, government attitude toward foreign assistance was a combination of optimism and caution. As the planning Commission noted;[4]

> external assistance is acceptable only if it carries with it no conditions, explicit or implicit, which might affect even remotely the country's ability to take an **independent line in international affairs**. There are also obvious risks in excessive reliance on foreign aid, which depends on the domestic political situation in lending countries and which might be interrupted by any untoward international developments. Yet, the commission felt, external resources at strategic points and stages can be of so much assistance in a period of rapid development that it is desirable, consistently with other objectives, to create conditions favorable to their inflow.

The anxiety was, clearly, to ensure that the country's policy of non-alignment remained non-negotiable i.e. free from the purview of aid transactions. That no aid would be worth a compromise on this policy stand was vigorously proclaimed by Nehru.[5]

> There have been times when one word from us would have brought us many good things of life. We preferred not to give that word. If at any time help from abroad depends upon a variation, howsoever slight, in our policy we shall relinquish that help completely and prefer starvation and privation to taking such help.

To counterbalance this self-denying idealism, Nehru also had a pragmatic strategy to count upon. In his words again; [6]

> We want the help of other countries and are going to get it too in a large measure... in accepting economic help or in getting political help; it is not a wise policy to put all your eggs in one basket.

A diversified base of economic aid from abroad was thus supposed to minimise the likely impact of such aid on the autonomy of the country's foreign policy. By implication, therefore, acceptance of aid from all willing quarters irrespective of any ideological animosity among the donors was believed to be compatible with the elite view of non-alignment. How and why donors antagonistic to each other would develop a common interest in India's development was not, however, clear in this formulation.

There is good authority to assume that this was not at least a calculated pay-off that the authorities thought would be flowing from non-alignment itself. As Krishna Menon, one of the architects and vociferous advocate of non-alignment, admitted, in reply to the question if "non alignment was thought of as the most efficient path to economic development".

> I don't think anyone thought about it that way at the time, because the question of foreign aid and things of that kind, which are so prominent today, did not figure in our minds very much. We didn't think back from economics to politics.[7]

The pay-off however, was there in a latent form and was visible only around the mid-fifties when the Soviet Union started taking substantial interest in India's economic development.[8] In the meanwhile development assistance to India was coming mainly from Western sources, and it is common knowledge why the United States had taken a leading role in the matter. That the motive of the United States was far from altruistic should be plain from a perusal of the public papers of the American Presidents. Thus in his address on Mutual Security Programme, President Truman stated"[9]

> Since the shadow of communist control has darkened China, India stands as the largest democratic nation in all Asia. But India is faced with the same kind of threat which overpowered the Chinese. We have a chance to help stop that threat in India not by sending guns and planes, but by...our program of economic and technical assistance.

> The next President, Eisenhower, wrote to the Senate Appropriations Committee:[10]

> I wish also to emphasize the importance of economic and technical assistance for the Near East, for India and Pakistan...these programs, many of which require only modest amounts of money, are an integral part of our program for **America's security**.

So, American aid to India's development was not predicated upon any relaxation of her non-alignment, notwithstanding the proverbial Dulles dispensation about its immorality. The decisive factor was the unmistakably non-communist character of the Indian government whose records at home in the context of the Telengana uprisings and acquiescence in the transit of Gurkha regiments for British counter-insurgency operations in Malay were certainly reassuring.[11] Even Prime Minister Nehru could refrain from making an oblique reference to this bait of anti-communism when he addressed the National Foreign Trade Council and Far East America Council of Commerce and Industry[12] during his first visit to the USA:

> We do not wish to rely needlessly on external help ...But there are certain essential things which, if we do not get them now, will delay our program.... And it makes a great difference in the present context when **other events**, totally unrelated to the peculiar problem before us, **other events in India, in Asia, in the world**, are somehow setting the pace. Therefore it becomes doubly necessary for us to make good on the economic front.

The whole scenario, however, underwent interesting transformation when Soviet leaders, on the eve of their Asian tour, threw open the challenge of competitive coexistence and expressed their determination "to prove the superiority of our system.[13] Almost instantly, donor motivation on the American side and recipient reaction on the Indian side were adjusted to this new development. For the first time, India's Five Year Plan came to enjoy simultaneous and substantial aid from both East and West. Summing up this phenomenon, Wilfred Malenbaum wrote in a Research Report[14] sponsored by American National Planning Association:

> India seems to be one of the few underdeveloped countries where both the United States and the U.S.S.R. maintain aid programmes significant in terms of the country's estimated requirements. These evidences of the coexistence of East and West in Indian economic and political life bear testimony to the skill with which leaders of India have conducted its domestic policy and international relations...indeed , both American and Russian involvement in India's economic affairs has tended to grow; India's non alignment has not impaired such expansion.

In other words , India was now going to be a convenient arena of contest for the two super powers each competing with economic aid to buy her political loyalty. Thus while non alignment was showing signs of pay-off on the economic front, it was also being put to harder political test of withstanding the pressures of cold war. As aid recipient, Indian authorities thought that the moment had come for them to exploit the equilibrium symbolised by the Super Power relations of coexistence. Geoffrey Tyson's comment[15] on this point is worth quoting:

> Nehru's political neutralism has now been extended to the economic sphere where its practical applications meant that India will consider herself free to accept assistance of every kind from the communist world without prejudice to her relations with the West.

It should be recalled, however, that freedom to choose the source of assistance is an essential ingredient to the autonomous pursuit of foreign relations and it was not this freedom that had the chance of being arrested at any time or for any reason. It was rather the increased economic dependence that constituted the main concern, the moot question being: how far availability of alternative sources of aid could really diversify and lessen the magnitude of this dependence.

Lessons of the Second Plan were certainly discouraging on this point. With its enormous outlay of Rs 4800 crore and an estimated 16.6% external assistance of Rs. 800 crore the Plan ultimately foundered on a mounting balance of payment crisis. Having subjected the plan to a searching mid-term appraisal (May 1958) and a thorough rephasing of its allocation, the Planning Commission came to the conclusion:[16]

> ... the balance of payments deficit over the plan period is expected to be of the order of Rs 2000 crores. Roughly one half of this deficit... incurred so far brought down the sterling balance held by the Reserve bank ... at about Rs 180 crores. And it is necessary to avoid drawing them down any further. For bridging over the estimated foreign exchange gap for the period October. 1958 to March 1959 external assistance totalling $350 million has been promised. The further assistance required for the rest of the plan period is estimated at $ 650 million, and this has yet to be secured . . . . It should also be noted that in estimating the foreign

exchange gap just mentioned it is assumed that no food imports over and above 'normal' purchases and existing commitments will be sanctioned unless covered by separate aid programmes.

Within the first decade of planning therefore, the extent of aid dependence encountered by the country was fully underlined. It arose not merely out of the magnitude or ambitiousness of the plan but also from several connected as well as extraneous factors. There was first the higher ratio of import over export bringing foreign exchange reserves down to a dangerously low level and thereby turning a substantial part of foreign aid into a fund for redressing payment imbalance. Secondly, an additional scarcity sector i.e food now emerged a claimant of special aid programmes. Aid dependence arising initially from capital requirement of economic growth thus came to be compounded by the common travails of a backward economy In a situation like this reliance on foreign capital aid does not diminish but increases over time and in the long run upsets all previous calculations about its safe handling

While the long term wisdom of the heavy industry bias in the second plan to meet the country's urgent needs for the basic infra-structure of development [17] cannot be disputed, it should be appreciated that when a development plan is undertaken without adequate mobilisation of domestic resources and little built-in safeguards for a likely trade imbalance there is no escape from aid dependence. For India the last resort for hard currency aid and commodity assistance being still held out by USA her economic future at least for some time came to be entwined with the interests and outlook of American decision makers Evidently there was a good deal of reservation in American political circles about giving aid to a country which was intolerably critical of U.S. alliance network in West and southeast Asia and was even accused of following a double standard in the case of Suez and Hungary. In strict economic terms , the very philosophy of planning in India came under sharp attack-so that a sympathetic president Kennedy had to plead the Indian case before the Senate:[18]

> It is easy to dismiss India's needs with the assertion that she has launched a pretentious and impossibly large scheme calling for a scale of effort and

> cumulative capital infusion wholly beyond her capacity. Yet is this so? Hardly. When we consider that the plan has a level of less than $7 per year per head and when we lay it beside the contemporary effort at totalitarian planning being made by China .... If the Second Plan collapses so may democratic India and the democratic hope in all of Asia setting in motion forces which would erode the broad security interests of the United States and its allies and result in a climate of blighted expectation the outcome of which has perhaps already been foreshadowed in the Indian State of Kerala where educated but despairing citizens freely elected a communist government.

With regard to the sudden spurt in Soviet in assistance to India , especially in the steel, mining, thermal power and heavy engineering sectors making India an admiring recipient of Russian technology, Kennedy believed that "Soviet assistance (was) largely confined to inflexible prestige projects " which compared to the diffused aid flowing from the west' "contribute (d) far less directly to human condition in India " and looked upon the situation as "an extraordinary opportunity to match systems with the Soviet union on favorable terms ... and to push India well ahead in its competition with the Chinese economy"[19]

Whereas the President's mind was preoccupied with the "China Syndrome," the dispensers of aid within the U.S. government and representing it on international agencies had been largely worked up by the Socialist syndrome in Indian planning. Illustrative of this are the views expressed by the Clay Committee Report on USAID:[20]

> We believe that U.S. should not aid a foreign government in projects establishing government owned industrial and commercial enterprises which compete with existing private endeavors. While we realize that in aiding foreign countries we cannot insist upon the establishment of our economic system.....we should not extend aid which is inconsistent with our beliefs, democratic tradition and knowledge of economic organization and consequences.

Elsewhere, at the Colombo Plan meetings, the same burden was repeated. As recounted by I.G Patel, a very senior official in the Union Ministry of Finance who represented the Indian government in many international negotiations:[21]

> I can still recall vividly the Colombo Plan meeting in New Zealand in 1956 where the British and the Americans in particular were sharply critical of our plans and policies. The meeting of the Colombo Plan took place soon after the Suez crisis and at a time when we had incorporated many features in our economic plans such as... acceptance of socialism and aid from socialist countries and emphasis on basic industries which were all anathema to many influential persons in the Western world then.

Commenting on the Aid India Consortium which was sponsored in 1958 under the auspices of World Bank Patel says;

> The Consortium being perhaps as rescue operation. But it soon emerged as a forum for getting our plans endorsed by the donor countries as a first step toward having their foreign exchange requirements underwritten jointly by the member of the group. The Second Plan had to be cut to the core midstrem.[22]

Earlier the world bank had sent a mission headed by Thomas H. McKittrick (April-June 1956)to examine the content of the Second Plan. The mission was critical of the ambitious investment in the public sector undermining the potentiality of private enterprise. Taking the criticism further the bank president Eugene Black issued a virtual note of warning which made "the pace and scale of our bank's further lone operation in India " contingent upon "the economic policies pursued by (Indian) government" Naturally the finance Minister of India politely retorted "We are of course not convinced that the motive of private profit is the only one which can ensure efficient operation in industry; nor do we believe that private enterprise is inherently superior to State enterprise."[23]

The issue came to a head over American participation in the development of India's fourth steel plant at Bokaro. Originally a brain child of George Woods, an influential banker who later headed the World Bank, the idea was to start an "impact project" to match Soviet-aided Bhilai. The long drawn public argument in which president Kennedy fought a losing battle[24] ultimately ended in scrapping of the item from 1963-64 U.S. Aid Bill. It remained a standing reminder to India of the extent to which donor pressures may be carried to influence the very course of her economic development, costing a time span of four years to get the project re-started. As the Soviets come to rescue, the American Ambassador to India John Kenneth Galbraith wrote in his diary :[25]

> Our past help to private sector plans such as Tatas, has evoked the comment ,"The Americans help the Tatas and Birlas who are already rich. By contrast, the Soviets . . . build plants that belong to the people. "

Of course the Bokaro episode did not rupture American aid relations with India . On the contrary the U.S. government was contemplating to send an international joint mission to weave together the various aid programmes of the western nations for the Third Five year plan. [26] A sense of urgency was added to U.S. concern for India in the aftermath of the Chinese invasion (October 1962), which made President Kennedy recommend to the Congress "additional efforts on our part to help bolster the security of this crucial area."[27] Security concerns now came to compound India's aid dependence and were reflected in her readiness to receive Western military aid. Of course this did not require a formal renunciation by India of her policy of non-alignment , though great tempo was noticed in public debates concerning the pros and cons of such a policy.[28] All that it entailed was the acceptance of a non-doctrinaire perspective for the future application of non-alignment . With the onset of a new era of understanding between the Super Powers to which was juxtaposed a new cold war between Moscow and Peking Indian leaders found it easier to move towards an equal proximity view of non-alignment vis-a-vis USA and USSR. Hence the period that followed was in many ways going to be a period of trial for the relative disinterestedness in donor behavior of USA and USSR vis-a-vis the policies India wanted to pursue in foreign as well as internal affairs. The outcome of this trial would largely determine if there was going to be any narrowing of the distance in favour of either super power — a distance which Indian leadership had been so long at pains to keep equal. A non-doctrinaire approach to feign policy would thus mean an assessment of the complementarity , or the lack of it, between the national interests of India and those of the major powers to whom the policy is addressed

The question of aided development apart, this assessment of complementarity assumed great urgency because of the new vulnerabilities that came to plague the country increasingly in the sixties.

These arose from a persistent agricultural shortfall making it difficult for the authorities to feed the country's teeming millions. Side by side, there was the sombre situation on the country's borders which after the 1962 debacle lay dangerously open to foreign aggression. Since in the procurement of both food and ammunition, Indian authorities were getting accustomed to relief consignments form abroad, mostly from the West, they were heading towards a few more sobering experiences as to how progammes for defence development and even food for the people could be jeopardised by the arms-twisting tactics of the donor powers who would not relent short of proof positive of policy compliance. The impending danger was, no doubt, foreseen by Nehru a few months before his death as he told the Lok Sabha :[29]

> Real freedom is . . . economic freedom in the sense that you do not have to rely on other courtiers. You are friends with them you take their help but you are not dependent upon them to carry for defense or anything else.

Yet Nehru did not have to work out or face the full implication of this stand in the sphere of foreign policy. For one thing the atmosphere of competitive coexistence between the major powers considerably eased the complexity of such exercise. For, one power bloc would not knowingly walk out of a prize area to be happily embraced by another. More important, during Nehru's premiership India's reliance on outside assistance cannot be said to have assumed a magnitude sufficient to menace her economic and political independence. Total foreign Ioan and grants as percentage of investment outlay during the first three plans (of which the Third was not even half-way through when Nehru died) stood at 5.8,13.2ánd 19.4 respectively.[30] The real dangers of external assistance, viz. inordinate burden of debt servicing and actual or threatened termination of aid affecting crucial moment of national policy, were yet to raise their heads. And when they actually did one would not know how far the safeguard for such a contingency, which in Nehru's mind simply lay in not putting "all one's eggs in one basket " would have really bailed the country out . The actual seriousness of the pinch was felt by post-Nehru administrators when the county had to encounter a full-scale war with Pakistan (1965) even before she had recovered from the Chinese attack. On the one hand, the Soviet Union in an obvious bid to wean over the pro-Chinese authorities of Pakistan was found retracing its earlier unequivocal support for India on questions like Kashmir and trying to get even handed with both nations on the subcontinent. As M.S. Rajan observed:[31]

> Indians were a little surprised at the Soviet Union's neutrality in the Indo-Pakistani conflict of September 1965 and scrupulous impartiality in the Tashkent negotiation (January 1966) between India and Pakistan —*surprised* because Pakistan was a member of the western camp and India was nonaligned and more friendly to the Soviet Union. The circle become complete when recently the Soviet Union in effect stepped into the breach created by the withdrawal of American Military assistance to Pakistan. The Soviet assistance is presumably meant to reduce Pakistan's dependence on China for arms, but, ask Indians, against whose threat to Pakistan's security?

More grievous was the American decision to suspend all economic and military assistance to India on the self corrective pretext given by President Johnson in his special message to the Congress on February 1,1966 that "the USA" will not allow our aid "to subsidize an arms race between these two countries "[32] though it was common knowledge that American military assistance to Pakistan was being used in clear contravention of President Eisenhower's pledge to Prime Minister Nehru that the aid would not be "directed in any way against India "[33] While apparently the U.S. government was within its right to delink its arms supply from the tension–prone subcontinent, its timing of the suspension of food supplies could not but appear as an act of arm-twisting.

Reliance on American supply of grains which thus happened to accentuate the country's vulnerability to external manipulation was begun in the fifties as a measure of insurance against the danger of rise in food prices such as could upset the course of economic development.[34] That this was not going to be just a one –way traffic was clear from President Eisenhower's budget message[35] which admitted that "this program was predicated upon adoption of our domestic agricultural program which should not involve the continued accumulation of large surplus" Besides under the Agricultural Commodities Agreement of August 28,1956, only U.S, flag vessels were to be used for the shipment of the commodities and the rupee balances accruing from freight payment and disposal of imported food would be used partly for U.S. aid to India's economic development and partly for U.S government's own use in India. The quantum of commodity flow was further augmented with the signing of the long-term Food for Peace Program (1960) said to be "four times as large as any agreement previously signed . . .since 1956"[36] Contrary to expectations, the outcome of the programme was thoroughly dismal. It had the effect of dampening agrarian incentives in India which resulted in repeated crop failures compelling further import of food grains Between the period 1961-62 and 1965-66 India's wheat import bill rose form Rs 939 crores while at the same time the government had to incur substantial losses to market the imported food at subsidized prices .[37a]

So far as the utilization of the rupee balance is concerned, they remained mostly unutilized and went on multiplying as Indian repayments on loans and deposits came to accrue to the American counterpart fund.[37b] In the long run therefore, American commodity assistance was producing a double jeopardy for India by inducing a sycophancy on the production front and imposing a revolving indebtedness for what was seemingly received as an outright grant. To put it softly, PL-480food programme made India dance to the tune of the "same song being sung twice over."[38]

The measure of vulnerability that grew from this near habitual dependence on the food front was even more sharply reflected on the country's balance of payments position Extended import commitment coupled with export shortfall and increasing burden of debt servicing forced a precarious sliding of the balance of payments. On account of total current and capital transactions, the average annual deposit for the Third Plan period stood at Rs 615 crores (=$1291.5)[39] The stage was thus prepared for an abject surrender to international pressures for devaluation of the Rupee to the extent of 57.5% in relation to U.S. dollar and the sterling. Even the Indian business community with its unmarred reputation of being pro-West had to realize:[40]

"This unwelcome decision stunned the entire nation and made it realize that it had been living beyond its means that it had to put the house in order and that it was dangerous to depend unduly on foreign countries for economic and other aids"

Whatever the economic justification of devaluation there is no gainsaying the fact that the decision to conform to I.M.F. directive was the cumulative effect of an international tutelage to which the Indian economic plans had been submitted. As the Planning Commission was busy formulating the Fourth plan on the basis of an extended foreign assistance covering about one-fourth of the total outlay (roughly $1.6 billion per annum),[41] the aid givers took another dose of liberty to scrutinize the soundness of the Fourth Plan. An Economic Mission of the World Bank headed by Bernard R. Bell produced a detailed critique of the institutional strategy and distributive objects of Indian planning. Its package recommendations included farmer incentive instead of cooperative approach to agricultural programe, relaxation of individual licensing to make room foreign private investment and an import liberalization program, all in the general background of a substinually devalued Rupee.[42] Since the package implied a virtual retreat from the social goals of planning hitherto upheld by Indian statesman, it created serious differences of opinion within the Union Cabinet and the Planning Commission. But presented as it was to a new and insecure government (under Lal Bahadur Shastri, subsequently succeeded by Mrs Gandhi) it was almost certain to exact conformity which under the circumstances was hard to distinguish from capitulation.[43] In the heat of the controversy that raged parliamentarians of all political affiliations, the government planning admitted that it had to act as it did "as all further aid negotiations hinged on it", and that "without reasonable prospects of aid forthcoming on the scale contemplated by us, the finalization of the Fourth Plan will be still further postponed."[44]

The plan was, indeed, postponed. What happened in its place was the announcement of a 'plan holiday' for three years through 1969. At the same time, India's request for food aid was easily converted into a control handle as President Johnson chose to adopt a "short tether policy" to release food on a month to month basis just to make sure that "India changed its farm policy".[45]

This was also the period when India had to maintain a very low profile in world politics. As Werner Levi[46] put it:

> ......under any circumstances India lacked the resources of a foreign policy commensurate with her ambitions...the growing need for aid from abroad ,especially food, began seriously to affect the substances of foreign policy and dictate the remaining content. Any separation of foreign

policy from foreign aid, attempted at an earlier period, proved unfeasible for many reasons, prominent among them increasing reluctance of aid donors to accept Indian political antagonism.

To India, the problem, however, was not one of her reduced freedom to criticize other powers For, even during the worst period of national crisis, Prime Minister Lal Bahadur Shastri evinced 'an unusual excess of clarity' in condemning American bombing of North Vietnam.* The public utterances of his successor on this and other related issues (Czechoslovakia not excepted) are also fairly well known. In fact the crux of the matter lay elsewhere. It should be traced to the new threat perception which Indian statesmen could ill afford to ignore in respect of dependence on foreign assistance. Y.B. Chavan who had the unique experience of running the ministries of Defence, Home, Finance and Foreign Affairs at different times ably summed up the position:

> If the threat to our national independence, inherent in excessive reliance on 'concessional' borrowing from abroad becomes apparent during 1965 when, despite our being a victim of Pakistani aggression, aid from most quarters was suspended, events in 1971 brought out even more forcefully that for **some countries at any rate** aid is still an instrument of interference in the politics of others.

The reference here is to the agonizing circumstances of Bangladesh crisis (1971) which put unprecedented strains on Indo-American relations and brought India closer to Soviet Union, diplomatically, militarily and economically. While the international issues surrounding the crisis encompassed grave and far-reaching considerations such as Super Power reactions to the turmoil's on the subcontinent portending dismemberment of Pakistan which then stood on the axis between Washington and Peking and heralding emergence of India as holder of the balance on the subcontinent, the question before India was fairly simple and decisive: whether, in the event of a showdown with Pakistan — which was inevitable if there was no satisfactory solution to the immediate problem of refugee

---

* Expression used in *'A Helpful Snub'*, a signed editorial by NJN in the Times of India, April 26,1965.

influx from East Pakistan and the ultimate problem of the political self-determination of Bangladesh, India could defend her legitimate interests as the central power on the subcontinent without adverse intervention from outside. Her worst fears took shape in the course of her protracted diplomatic tussle[47] with the USA and prompted her to buy a timely insurance for security with the Soviet Union (Indo-Soviet Treaty of Friendship, August 9, 1971). As war broke out between India and Pakistan with the latter launching a surprise air raid on December 3, 1971, the Nixon administration shed its neutrality in favour of its CENTO Ally by suspending all aid to India, dispatching the U.S, carrier the **Enterprise** close to the zone of hostilities and an all-out offensive in the United Nations against the policies and actions of the Indian Government.

Eventually, these unfriendly gestures proved counterproductive. Even the withholding of aid did not have debilitating effects on the Indian economy, partly due to the liberal assistance it was promised from alternative sources in Eastern Europe. But politically it had the remarkable effect of producing a strong will to self-reliance; for, the 1971 crisis was the first of its kind when India as an aid recipient could successfully thwart the pressure tactics of its largest aid –giver and make it eventually ask for restoration of normalcy on her own term. In his fourth Annual report to the Congress on U.S Foreign Policy, [48] President Nixon admitted:

> India emerged from the 1971 crisis with new confidence, power and responsibilities. This fact in itself was a new political reality for the subcontinent and for all nations concerned with South Asia's future.... The United States respects India in accordance with its new stature and responsibilities...India's relationship with the major powers are for it to decide, and we have no interest in inhibiting their growth...we can deal with each other now without sentimentality and without the illusions that because we are both great democracies our foreign policies must be the same.

If this meant a change in donor expectation of a pliable leadership in the recipient country and the beginning of a more mature relationship between the two, it called for a more astute handling of foreign aid by the Indian decision makers. For, from now on, the "largest democracy" appeal of a non-communist political leadership in India would not cut much ice against the frigid aid-weariness of the U.S.A .; acceptance of an increasing dose of assistance from the Soviet Union also would not stir it on to a course of competitive charity. The resultant shortfall, if any, in the quantum of foreign aid she will still need must be made good by approaching other donors who look for an economic rather than political return to their aid investment. On the whole, therefore, one would expect a progressive depoliticization of whatever economic aid India will be able to collect for her future development programmes — which in turn, would also entail a new responsibility for the Indian leadership to find ways and means to minimize the economic costs of foreign assistance.

II. Counter-Dependence Measures

The political implications of India's aid –dependence, as narrated above should not divert one's attention from the incontrovertible fact that what passed for aid was not charity but repayable loans with myriad strings about their utilization and that the actual debt servicing obligations of the country had been mounting from $191 million in 1961-62 to $ 506 million in 1969-70. Naturally one could not sit tight over the problem without plunging the Country into untold peril.

An assessment of this kind which was not too dissimilar from the position already taken by the opposition, both right and left, and also corroborated by public opinion surveys,[49] clearly presaged some serious thinking about the necessity of re-structuring the country's economic linkages with the outside world so that foreign assistance ,as long as it cannot be totally renounced , had the least damaging effect on the country's political and economic sovereignty. On the economic front it called for a number of strategies that had necessary and far-reaching effects in terms of the political distance or proximity the nation could usefully cultivate with each other. To begin with, there was to be a progressive reduction of the foreign aid content of the future Five Year Plans. The following table would illustrate the urgency with which this has been effected.

Table 3.1: Share of Foreign Assistance to plan Finance (Rs. Crores)

Plan Period	Total Outlay Public Sector)	Amount of Assistance	(3) as% of (2)
(1)	(2)	(3)	(4)
First Plan (51-56)	1960	189	9
Second Plan (56-61)	4672	1049	22.5
Third Plan (61-66)	8577	2423	28.3
Annual Plans (66-69)	6756	2426	35.9
Fourth Plan	16160	2087	12.9
Fifth Plan	37250	2443	6.4

Source: 1 *India Pocket Book of Economic information* 1972

2 *India*, 1974 p, 161

3 *Draft Fifth Plan* vol.I, pp 53-54,57

If the dwindling share of external assistance in India's development plans indicated aid-weariness of the donors it also served well to make the plans less and less aid propelled. From the Third Plan peak of 28.3% the percentage of net external assistance has descended to a bare 6.4% in the Fifth plan period.

Along with this phasing out of external assistance care had to be taken that the remaining part of this dependence was redistributed on a purely cost –benefit calculation. Since a large part of the aid was no better than commercial loans to be paid back with interest, it was considered wiser to borrow from sources interested in purely commercial transaction than those looking for a political *Quid pro Quo* on top of usual financial return.

One way of doing this was to cultivate closer association with the Soviet world for which little political price had ever to be paid by the country.[50] Contrary opinion widely shared in the West, must be weighed against the logic one finds in the following episode related by Prime Minister Mrs. Gandhi: [51]

> On one occasion, the American Ambassador complained to me that we had supported the Soviet Union on more occasions in the United Nations than we had supported other countries. I said ..."if you look at occasions on which we have seemed to side with the Soviet Union, what do you find? Were they not issues in which India and the developing

> countries were vitally interested? And if this was so, would it not be more true to say that the Soviet Union had supported the stand taken by the developing countries..and not that we had gone out of our way to support the Soviet Union?"

On the contrary, two outstanding instances in which India did resist Soviet political pressure were adherence to the NPT and the Brezhnev plan for an Asian Collective Security.

Politics apart, Soviet aid has its appeal on purely economic considerations too. Released against specific projects for development of key industries, the aid becomes self liquidating through a prudent combination of Rupee payment import of capital goods by India, Soviet purchases of Indian merchandise of special export interest and Rupee-serviced debt obligations spread out over a long period and repayable at a soft interest rate of 2.5%. In the long run, it is these advantages[52] that accounted for the growing flow of assistance from the East European countries.

At the same time one cannot gloss over the fact that aid from the East European sources was yet to reach a magnitude sufficient to counterbalance the existing level of aid from the major Western powers. As the statistics show, the Soviet Union lagged far behind the U.S percentage of 38.2% to the total aid received by India from different sources upon March 1975. In fact it would be a tall order to hope to make up any substantial loss of aid India may sustain from the non-Communist world by corresponding gains from the Communist world.

A third line of defence , therefore , consists in enhancing the harvest of bilateral agreements with developed Western countries who do not manifestly entertain any global political ambitions and have seldom, if ever ,tried to interfere with the domestic and external policies of India. Countries belonging to this category take their rank in the following order: West Germany, France, Norway, Sweden and Denmark (see table 3.3).With Japan joining this list from the Asian continent and warmer relations envisaged with Canada and UK, India finds herself back again to the oasis of foreign assistance with the added advantage that this time she has acquired the necessary wisdom and some ability to choose for herself how much, from whom and at what cost. In any case, there can be no comfort regarding the amount of debt servicing the country has been shouldering since the launching of her Five Year Plans. As illustrated by Table 3.2, annual outflow on account of debt servicing has now assumed menacing proportions eating up about 27% of the country's present level of export earning and exceeding 50% of the gross aid inflow in recent times. Hence India must not only make sure that she gets more than she pays out but also obtain aid on less stringent terms.

Table 3.2: Gross & Net Inflow of External Assistance into India
1951/2 to 1970/1 ($mn)

	1951/2-1955/6 1st Plan	1956/7-1960/1 2nd Plan	1961/2-1956/6 3rd Plan	1966/7-1968/9 Ann. Plan	1969/70-1970/1 4th Plan
1. Gross aid utilized	413	1,860	4,232	4,296	2,156
2. Repayments	50	251	1,141	1,2432	1,056
a. Amortization	na	na	643	745	656
b. Interest	na	na	498	498	400
3. Net aid (1-2)	363	1,609	3,091	3,053	1,100
Net aid as % of Gross aid	87.8	86.5	73.0	71.1	51.0
Repayments as % exports	0.8	3.9	14.3	25.0	26.9

Source : Govt. of India: Economic Survey

As a further guarantee against any embarrassment or disappointment to her quest for aid, she in combination with the Group of 77, has succeeded in inducing quite a few stabilizing changes in the role of the donors. There is, first, the pledge, gradually redeemable but nonetheless irreversible, on the part of the developed countries to part with at least 1% of their GNP for the advancement of the developing countries. Second, there has been an agreement for progressive softening of the terms of loan, including re-scheduling of debt servicing and refinancing in appropriate cases. Third, an organic link, though at an embryonic stage at the moment has been established between the requirements of economic growth of the developing countries and the preferential or concessional treatment of their trade with the developed world.[53] Fourth in recent times she has been able to elicit a favorable response from the Fund-Bank Development Committee to have as much as 40% of the

IDA funds allocated in her favour. After all, she has all along placed her best hopes of development on international cooperation flowing from multilateral agencies where she can hopefully use her membership to neutralize any political conditions being attached to the grant of aid.[54] Fifth and most important of all, in the field of foreign trade she has moved through thick and thin into a position which certainly gives her unprecedented strength to negotiate aid with others. With export rising at 10.9% and import consequently liberalized, the foreign exchange reserves of the country stood at Rs 3200 Crores at the start of the finical year 1977-78-a more than fourfold increase between March 1975 and March 1977. In fact, in 1977-78 India did not draw from the IMF but made repayments totaling Rs 300 Crores against 1974 drawings.[55] The cumulative effect of all this is a sense of optimism and self confidence which makes the then Union Finance Minister, Mr H.M Patel feel "no need to allow a free import of foreign capital or knowhow" or to seek aid except through multilateral agencies, [56]

Last but not least , mention must be made of the new machinery India has developed for ensuring techno economic collaboration with foreign countries on a reciprocal basis, so that external assistance no longer looks like a one we-way traffic. Starting with the Indo-Czech Joint Committee in 1966, India now has established high-level Joint Commissions not only with the developed market and socialist economics but also with a number of developing countries in Asia and Africa. In the appraisal of the External Affairs Ministry; [57]

These Commissions serve a useful purpose by transcending bilateral agreements with a given country and providing a sort of supreme review body or an overall 'umbrella' to oversee, accelerate and coordinate the activities of the various existing bilateral agreements besides indentifying, from its vantage point, additional fields of cooperation in keeping with the changing needs of industrial and commercial developments.

The frequency with which these Commissions will work, the variety and depth of agenda with which they will deal and, above all, the atmosphere of mutual trust that they will generate in an interlocking arrangements of economic cooperation-are some of the factors which will definitely make them a great institutional innovation in the ordering of India's diplomacy.

Table 3.3: External Assistance to India by major donors & types, 1951/2 to 1970/1 (Rs. mn)

	1st Plan 1951/2-1955/6		2nd Plan 1956/7-1960/6		3rd Plan 1961/2-1965		Ann. Plans1 1966/7-1968/9		4th Plan 1969/70-1970/1		Total 1951/2-1970/1		% of Total utiliz-ed Aid 1951/2-1970/1	Utilised aid as % autho-rised 1951/2-1970/1
	Auth	Util	Auth	Util	Auth	Util	Auth	Util	Auth	Util	Auth	Util		
1. Loans	2,268	1,264	12,813	7,247	23,290	19,070	22,396	22,005	12,023	13,902	72,790	63,488	68.6	87.2
a. Repayable in foreign currencies	2,122	1,240	10,509	6,079	22,830	17,514	22,261	21,796	12,020	13,900	69,742	60,529	65.4	86.8
(i) Multilateral loans	572	338	2,612	2,228	4,116	3,240	3,547	4,249	2,744	1,878	13,591	11,933	12.9	87.8
(ii) Bilateral loans	1,550	903	7,897	3,851	18,714	14,274	18,714	17,547	9,276	12,022	56,151	48,597	52.5	86.5
1. USA	903	903	1,085	368	7,732	6,389	8,443	7,737	4,150	5,149	22,313	20,546	22.2	92.1
2. West Germany	-	-	-	-	3,080	2,197	1,351	1,873	1,149	1,077	5,580	5,147	5.6	92.2
3. UK	-	-	1,226	1,218	2,420	1,704	1,893	2,237	1,829	1,564	7,368	6,723	7.3	91.2
4. Japan	-	-	268	160	1,380	883	875	1,223	243	482	2,766	2,748	2.9	99.3
5. USSR	647	-	3,190	748	1,005	2,073	2,584	1,365	-	863	7,426	5,049	5.5	68.0
6. Others	-	-	2,304	1,357	3,097	1,028	3,568	3,112	1,905	2,887	10,698	8,384	9.0	78.4
b. Repayable in rupees	146	23	2,304	1,168	460	1,562	135	209	3	2	3,048	2,964	3.2	97.2

2. Grants	1,380	702	1,212	1,603	1,325	1,062	1,661	2,258	923	817	6,501	6,442	6.9	99.1
1. USA	918	443	546	856	218	311	56	106	157	-	1,895	1,716	1.8	90.6
2. UK	4	-	4	4	10	8	53	55	38	39	109	106	0.1	97.2
3. Canada	323	197	571	603	851	544	1,194	1,675	427	487	3,366	3,506	3.8	104.1
4. Others	135	62	91	140	246	199	358	422	301	291	1,131	1,114	1.2	98.5
3. Other Assistance[3]	169	51	11,309	5,448	4,506	8,532	6,213	7,194	736	1,452	22,933	22,677	24.5	98.9
4. Total Assistance (1+2+3)	3,817	2,017	25,332	14,298	29,121	28,670	30,270	31,457	13,682	16,171	102,222	92,613	100.0	90.6
Utilized as % authorized	-	52.8	-	56.4	-	93.4	-	103.9	-	118.2	-	90.6	-	-
UK as % total	0.10	-	4.85	8.54	8.34	5.97	6.42	7.28	13.64	9.91	7.37	7.37	7.37	-

References

1. On early conflicts between the radical and the conservative wings of the Congress Party see Francine R Frankel, op. cit pp 71-77 and 84-94 Regarding Nehru's compromising role, see Gyan Chand, *Nehru and Planning* in Nehru Legacy: A Symposium by National Book Club, June 1966.
2. Till the '70 when conscious export promotion measures yielded, for the first time, positive results, the Indian economy was predominantly inward-looking its reliance being mainly on import prohibition and import substitution see Animesh Haldar, *India's Export Pattern: Analysis of Potential Diversification*, P27, Minerva, Calcutta, 1976
3. GOI, *Advisory Planning Board, Report (January 1947)*, paras 18 &20, pp 6-7, New Delhi
4. Planning Commission, GOI, *First Five Year Plan, P26.*
5. *Nehru, Speeches*, (1949-53), p222, voL II, GOI, Publications Division.
6. Ibid,, Vol 1 (1946-49), p 219.
7. Michael Brecher, *India and World Politics*, op, cit. pp3-4
8. For a brief review of the developments behind changing Soviet View of India from adverse indifference to warm friendship, see Harish Kapur, *India and the Soviet Union*, in K.P Misra (e.d) Foreign Policy of India: A Book of Readings, pp 242-249, Thomson Press India Ltd, New Delhi, 1977
9. *Public Papers of the Presidents of the United States*: Harry S.Truman, Radio and T.V, Address, March 6 1952, p 195 USGPO
10. ibid. *Eisenhower, Letter to Senate Appropriation Committee*, July 23, 1953, p 143 (emphasis added)
11. See Statement of the Communist Party of India, Calcutta Congress, Feburary 28, 1949, Also, Ajoy Ghosh (Secretary General, CPI), *Communist Answer to Pandit Nehru*, Delhi , CPI Pamphlets, cit, in Taufique Ahmed Nizami, *The Communist Party and India's Foreign Policy*, Associated, New Delhi 1971
12. Nehru, *Visit to America*, op.cit,pp 76-77
13. Pravda, December 30 1955
14. Wilfred Malenbaum, *East and West in India's Development: the Economics of Competitive Coexistence*, p 3, NPA, USA,1959
15. Geoffrey Tyson , *India and the Russian visitors, International Affairs*, April 1956,pp 173-180,RIIA,OUP, LONDON,1956.
16. GOI, Planning Commision, *Plan Resources and Outlay*: A Review, pp2-3, New Delhi, July 1959.
17. See Baldev Raj Nayyar, *The Modernization Imperative and Indian Planning*, pp 107-123, Vikas, Delhi 1972
18. Cit Ram Singh and M.K Haldar, *Kennedy through Indian Eyes*, p 102 Vir Publishing Delhi,1964.
19. ibid .pp 110-111
20. *Clay Committe Report*, cit Gustav Ranis, The United Statesand Developing Economics, New York,1964
21. I.G. Patel, *Foreign Aid, Lal Bhadur Shastri Memorial Lecture*, Institute of Public Enterprise, p 13, Allied, Bombay,1963.
22. ibid. p13
23. *The Hindu*,11 and 13 October,1956
24. News conference, May 8,1963, *Public papers of the President 1963*, p377.
25. J.K.Galbraith, *Ambassador's Journal*, p215, Houghton Miffin Boston 1969.

26. Kennedy's speech at committee for International Economic Growth, cit Singh and Haldar,op.cit,p 119
27. Message to congress,April 21963, *Public Papers of the President* ,1963, p299
28. See Rajni Kothari, *Indian Foreign Policy: Need for a Non-doctrinnaire Perspective* in A.B Shah (ed). India's Defence and foreign policies. Manaktales, Bombay;Cecil V Crabb (Jr). the testing of Nonalignment, *Western Political Quarterly*. vol17,September 1964, pp517-540. M.S Rajan, *Chinese Aggression and the Future of India's Non alignment Policy,* International Studies, vol5,july-october 1963 pp118-132. That the US itself was not interested in any kind of alliance with India which it found 'too expensive' is recorded in Galbraith op .cit. p 479.
29. *Lok Sabha Debates,* August 22,1963, Third Series, Vol 19, col 2197-98
30. *Estimates Committee (1967-68) Report to 4th* Lok Sabha, Ministry of Finance,Utilisation of External Assistance,pp 5-8, Lok Sabha sect, New Delhi,1967
31. M.S Rajan, *India in World Politics: Post Nehru Era,* international Journal XXIV, No 1,pp 138- 158,Toronto , 1968.
32. *Public papers of the US Presidents*: Lyndon B Johnson (1966), pp 122-123
33. *Public papers of the US Presidents*: Eisenhower (1954), letter to Nehru, Feburary 25,1954, p284.
34. Ministry of Finance, GOI, *Annual Report* 1956-57, p35
35. *Public papers of the US Presidents*: Eisenhower, Annual Budget Message, January 21, 1954,pp 139-40 (emphasis added)
36. ibid;Eisenhower (1960),p 397
37. (a) Sulekh Chandra Gupta, *Freedom from Foreign Food,* p61,Blitz National Forum, New Delhi,1965
37. (b) According to RBI estimate;the extent of US holding allocation wise: Loans/Grants to GOI... allocation % 79.9 of which balance

	held by USA...........Rs	248.8 crores
Cooley Loans	6.7...........................	47.5 "
U.S. uses	13.4........................	90.3 "
Other receipts	....	208.2 "
	Total balances----------	594.8 "

38. Little & Clifford, *International Aid,* Allen and Unwin, London 1965. Cit S Venu. *The Developing Economies and the The international Framework,* p 148, Orient Longman, Bombay 1971
39. Government of India, ECONOMIC SURVEY 1975-76, P 102 During the same period the percentage of food import to the total import bill stood between 19.5 and 25.6
40. *Journal of the Indian Merchants Chambers of Commerce,* LXI No1, p29,Bombay, January 1967.
41. *Times of India,* January 30,1965.
42. *Bell Report to President World Bank on India's Development Efforts,* VoL II –IV, October 1965.
43. See Frankel, op cit, pp 269-300.
44. Cit. Bhagawati, Jagdish N. and T.N Srinivasan, *Foreign Trade Regimes, and Economic Development of India,* p 8, Amsterdam Noth Holland Publishing CO, 1974
45. Lyndon B. Johnson, *The Vantage Point, perspectives of the Presidency,* pp 225-228, Hold Rinehart & Winston, New York,1971
46. Werner Levi, *Foreign Policy: The Shastri Era,* rep. in K.P Misra (ed) Studies in India Foreging Policy, p 190, Vikas ,New Delhi, 1969.

47. see Mrs Gandhi's correspondence and relevant portions of the *Anderson Papers* cit. Vinod Gupta, Anderson Papers: A study of Nixon's Blackmail of India , ISSD, New Delhi, 1972.
48. *Public Papers of the US President,* Nixon's Foreign policy statement to the Congress, M ay 3, 1973, pp 457-58.
49. See table in *Monthly Public Opinion Survey,* vol 15 December 1969 and August 1970.

Indian Attitudes towards Foreign Aid, 1969-79

				1969	1970
1	Q: ' Do you favour India getting aid from foreign countries?'				
	A: (%)	1 Favour strongly		22	22
		2 Favour Somewhat		39	39
		3 Oppose Somewhat		15	12
		4 Oppose strongly		18	20
		5 Doesn't matter; don't know		6	7
2	Q: Are you aware that India is getting aid from....?				
	A: (% who replied yes)		1 USA	96	98
			2 USSR	85	82
			3 UK	67	39
			4 WEST GERMANY	64	55
			5 JAPAN	64	61
3	Q: 'Has too great a price been paid for assistance?'				
	A: (%)	1 Too high rates of interest charged			47
		2 Excessive obligatiotions for short Period repayment			43
		3 Don't agree with either criticism 1 or 2			2
		4 Don't know			18
4	Q: Do you think the assistance has improved the standard of living or has it made little difference?'				
	A %	1 Improved		51	45
		2 little difference		43	46
		3 Don't Know		6	9

50. See Swarn Singh's reply to foreign affairs Debates in Lok Sabha, 27 December 1973, *Foreign Affairs Record,* December 1973, pp 506-16
51. Congress Party Seminar address August 31, 1970, rep, in *Speeches and Reminiscences of Indira Gandhi,* p 133, Rupa, Calcutta 1975
52. M. Sebastian Stanislaua, *Soviet Economic to India,* Chap 7 & 9, N.V Publications, New Delhi 1975, Pramit Chaudhuri *East European Aid to India in Deepak Nayyar* (ed) Economic Relations between Socialist Countries and the Third World, pp 142-161, Macmillan, London, 1977
53. See Shah M. Bijli, *Developing Nations and UNCTAD,* International Book Traders Aligarh-1973; S.M. Tawale *India's Economic Diplomacy* in the *United Nations,*Meenakshi Prakashan, Meerut, 1975, pp 145-190
54. Percentage shares of IBRD and IDA loans to the total aid received by India during 1974-75 stood at 9.6% and 43.4%.
55. H.S Chhabra (ed), *Indian Economic Diary,* vol VIII p 3285, New Delhi ,1977
56. ibid. p 5358
57. *GOI, MEA report* 1972-73, pp 75-76, New Delhi, 1976

4

A Mixed Economy's Endeavour for Growth Without Dependence

THE INDIAN ECONOMY, for the past three decades (19650's to 1980)has been subjected to a continuous process of planned restructuring under central direction. An interesting consequence of this effort has been the increasing infusion of a national political vision into the economic order. This progressive politicization of the economy is, however, only superficially comparable to a similar process in the modern variant of the market economy.[1] The latter, while receiving measured doses of state regulation in exchange of the legal support it needs and receives for its long term operation can also manage to exert an occasional back-lash on the state authorities through its own political support structure across the social spectrum.

This spectacle, much as it is attractive to the barons of private business in India , generally appears in a subdued from because of the mixed economy arrangement. Under this set-up the major macro-economic decisions such as allocation of scarce and strategic resources, choice of sectors for massive planned investment, pattern of technology assimilation and, above all ,the inflow and outflow of resources across other countries are mostly taken care of by the State and therefore, largely subject to the political perceptions of those who are in power. In this sense economic planning may be viewed as a necessary extension of national politics.

As discussed earlier, one of the preoccupations of planning in India relates to the question of dependence and its successful reversal. The terms in which dependency, actual or apprehended, is conceived relate primarily to the threat perception of the national elite. While these threat perceptions get articulated through public agencies full play is given to economic nationalism so that all the vital sectors of the economy are put on alert and unite in their efforts to offer an effective resistance. In building up this resistance the public authorities have to count upon the support of the business community whose response, in turn, would depend not only upon its own appreciation of the situation but also upon its habitual relations with the wielders of political power.

It is precisely in this context that business-government interaction should be regarded as an important dimension to the management of foreign economic relations. In fact in a country like India public policies intended to combat, reduce or reverse dependency are seldom conceivable without a substantial measure of cooperation from the business community. The latter's association with the policymaking process, therefore, deserves a full scale examination. For the purpose of the present study attention will be focused mainly on two sensitive areas of public policy namely, foreign trade and foreign investment.

I. The Framework of Business-Government Interaction in India

The framework of business-government interaction in India though not formalized until the "Mixed Economy" speech of Prime Minister Nehru in support of his Industrial policy Resolution of April 7,1948 has been evolving for quite some time in the backdrop of the national independence movement The reason why in the post independence scheme of things the state came to acquire a preponderant position vis-à-vis private business without encountering effective obstruction from the national bourgeoisie is embedded in the latter's historical association with the new ruling forces. The Indian businessmen, already accustomed to state control in various forms under the British rule, expected that post-independence application of the same regulatory instruments would shield their unfulfilled aspirations from the onslaught of foreign competitors. Their alignment with the Indian National Congress was so complete that they did not want to be recognized as a special entity during the constitutional negotiations with the Cripps mission about the modalities of transfer of power lest that should weaken the negotiating position of the Congress which had already been complicated by sectional representations. In a Press Communiqué dated April 1, 1942, G.L. Mehta, the then President of the Federation of Indian Chambers of Commerce and Industry, stated:

> "Political autonomy would, in fact, be of little value and significance unless it was such as to ensure economic Independence and enable full economic development of the country.[2]"

Since in the view of FICCI, "India's vital economic interests have been subordinated to those of Britain," it openly declared that these interests "demanded the establishment of a representative national government". In as much as the British leaders like Churchill were critical of the collusion of Indian business interests with the agitational policies of the Congress, the FICCI made no secret of the matter that Indian commercial organizations did not feel apologetic about the fact that they were an integral part of the national movement..."[3]

Even before independence was achieved FICCI appears to have made some serious thinking about " the issues of far-reaching importance" which must be settled by the incoming national government in regard to defense expenditure ,sterling balances, lease-land operations , economic implications of the Atlantic Charter, fiscal and commercial implications of the Anglo-American Treaty."[4]

Thus it was long since the Indian business community had begun swimming with the currents of political nationalism in India and had built up close rapport with the emerging political elite in the hope that the new state apparatus could be conveniently used to promote their economic interests. The protectionist measures of the Indian government in the early years of independence[5] showed that the wind was blowing in the expected directions. Eventually, through such radical measures as land reforms that would weaken the hold of the feudal forces on the national economy and an expanding commitment of the public exchequer to invest in economic overheads hitherto avoided by private capital, the state did provide an excellent springboard for the future ventures of capitalism in India.

The ground rules of this collaborative relation between the State and the private business interests were first laid down in the 1948 Industrial Policy Resolution and subsequently expanded in a new Resolution (April

30, 1956) Both envisaged sharing of economic activities between the two entities, though the latter was more definitive about the predominance of the State Sector. This system, usually known as 'mixed economy', would proceed not from an uncritical programme of nationalization of the existing industries most of which represented obsolete technology and, therefore, did not deserve huge public spending in compensation for nationalization. The strategy was rather one of acquisition of new technology and creation of new overheads by the State with a view to having a stronger grip over the whole economy. Normally this would not upset investment incentives or injure existing business interests in the private sector. In fact the captains of industry were assured by Nehru that "for at least ten years, may be more" the government would "not touch" the private undertaking[6] outside the high priority area reserved for public investment. Even the more ambitious 1956 Resolution which apart from making 17 basic and strategic industries the exclusive preserves of the state, raised the possibility of other essential industries and public utility services being "progressively State owned", also made it clear: "Inevitably there will not only be an area of overlapping but also a great deal of dovetailing between industries in the private and public sector."[7]

Two things, therefore, stood out in the period immediately following independence. First the Indian capitalists who had tough time developing an industrial base under the British rule had to utilize the pressures of national movement to extort concessions from the imperialist rulers.[8] Consequently there was not much of a likelihood of their developing an overly comprador attitude toward international monopoly capital. On the contrary, the growing sense of economic nationalism encouraged them to enter into positive interaction with the new elite in the national matters as well as international. Secondly, what made this interaction all the more worthwhile for the businessmen was the rewards they expected from a collaborative relation with the State which, as was promised, would not encroach upon the existing private enterprise but would rather surround it with a whole array of catalytic forces for expansion. As long as the State went on providing the basic industrial infra-structure, resource inputs and even long term finance[9] for the sustenance of the private sector, the latter would have every reason to remain a partner in the alliance.

This does not mean that those who command the private sector of the economy have had no quarrel with the authorities or that they cheerfully acquiesced in everything that the on-going planning process entailed for them. On the contrary as the mixed economy strategy came to be exploited in the name of a vaguely conceived socialism,[10] a good deal of resentment grew against the long arm tactics of the government. Businessmen in India not only resented the mushrooming of state regulations[11] and the attending mismanagement on the part of the bureaucracy[12] but harboured serious misgivings about the secondary role of the private vis-a-vis the public sector,[13] Also at times, they organized stout opposition to the radical measures of the government such as regulation of monopolies and restrictive trade practices[14] or dilution of the original guarantee of the right to property in the Constitution.[15] By far the most serious threat emanating from the government so far was posed by the Report of the Industrial Licensing Policy Enquiry Committee (1979)which recommended greater controlling powers for the government over the management of private enterprise on the ground that a substantial part of the finance required by private companies was being provided by government sponsored/owned financial institutions.[16] By and large, however, business-government interaction remains a matter of balancing the political convictions of the party in power with the entrenched interests of the private entrepreneurs. As long as the one does not push the other too hard, there is no reason why there should not be some sort of a mutual accommodation. In fact, barring the period of internal emergency from June 1975 to March 1977, there has been no occasion for the business interests in India to feel entirely uncertain or frustrated about a fair deal from the government as the necessary condition for this accommodation. The policies of the government, however radically worded, have not so far jeopardized the basic interests of the business community in India. On the contrary, the general outlook that has been developing over the period is one that regards private enterprise as 'a cooper ant factor' and the government as the 'pace setter' each having a stake in the programme of economic development.

This common stake is highlighted by a couple of plain facts connected with the economic reality of the country. First, the attitude of private enterprise in India toward the public sector is made up of mixed feelings and sways very much by the prevailing political climate. Thus the FICCI while usually demanding a revision of the official weightage in favour of the public sector in almost every five year plan, is also on record as:

"always taking the view... that the controversy over the sectoral issue is both meaningless and unnecessary"[17a] and that "policy decisions have generally been marked by a spirit of pragmatism."[17b] In a correspondence on Industrial Licensing policy Mr. S.L. Kirloskar, President of FICCI, wrote to the Planning Minister Ashok Mehta:[17c]

> I do appreciate that the implementation of the Industrial Policy Resolution has not been as rigid as it was once apprehended. Governments have endeavoured to keep in step with the requirements and needs of the country. The decision to permit private sector to participate effectively in the development of industries like pig iron, fertilizers, alloy steel, etc, is a case in point.

No less important is the consideration that the public sector in India is not growing at the cost of the private sector and the incidence of frequency of nationalization has been far from frightening. If after the takeover of life insurance business in the mid-fifties there was suddenly a wave of nationalization sweeping the industrial landscape between 1969 and 1974 it was warranted by the in fights that flared up between monopoly and non-monopoly bourgeoisie with its repercussions on national politics leading to the fragmentation of the Congress monolith.[18]

Secondly, occasional skirmishes involving the two sectors have seldom weakened the case for integrating their activities. The basic and the most convincing argument in this connection is that they both require continually expanding demand and preferably in complementary areas. To entrepreneurs in India an uneven partnership with the public sector is at most a minor irritant, for the benefits that the latter hold out for them far outweigh the usual inconveniences of 'big movement'. Apart from replenishment of their capital with long term advances from State financial agencies, [19] they have found the State undertakings to be quite an attractive source of industrial raw materials, technical inputs and specialized services.[20] This, in addition to their habitual dependence on the government as the bulk buyer of industrial output for the railways, defense and public works,[21] makes them retain a kind of symbiotic relationship with the State sector.

On the government side too, there is considerable awareness of the need to synchronize its economic policies with the climate of thinking in the business circles. Thus even at the height of the controversy about the feasible equation between public and the private sector, the Planning Commission went ahead with its scheduled meeting with a specially constituted committee of the FICCI to discuss the strategies and magnitude of investment during the Third Plan. Besides, the Ministry of Commerce and Industry have made it part of their routine to consult or send for written suggestions, of the FICCI on important matters like Export Promotion , opening of Free Trade Zones, multilateral tariff negotiations with the European Economic Community and also at the Kennedy Round. Besides, at least one FICCI representative has as a rule served on Indian delegations to international conferences on GATT and Intra-regional trade between ECAFE countries. [22] It does not also escape one's notice how the annual meetings of the FICCI and other commercial and professional interest groups in India are invariably inaugurated by one or the other State dignitary. No wonder that the transactions on such occasions are usually marked by reciprocal good counselling.

The foregoing details picked up at random from the recent economic history of the country, illustrate the common bond that has emerged between the private and the public sector in India during the last three decades the mixed economy model has been in operation. This makes the task of foreign policymaking a good deal easier for the authorities concerned. For instance , they can effectively transmit their calculation of expected benefits as well as threat perceptions in international economic diplomacy not only to the business community who may, accordingly, orient their projections about the priorities of production , choice of import –export channels, attitude towards foreign investment and technology transfer, and so on. This in turn immensely helps the government to undertake long range plans for forging new economic linkage with nations whose political outlook it finds to be not only the least troublesome but positively helpful to the pursuit of its international objectives.

The following two sections dealing with public polices about foreign trade and foreign investment should substantiate the contention that international economics of the country, in at least two major and sensitive areas, have been largely guided by business-government interaction at home.

II. New Channels of Trade to Redress the Old

It has been noted in the previous chapter that growing disenchantment with foreign assistance led the government since the mid-sixties to shift its emphasis from aid to trade as a more viable means to ensure capital goods import on usual commercial terms free from extraneous obligations. Indeed, freedom to choose the source as well as the content of such import is basic to the autonomy of national economic development. Growth of a country's foreign trade, however, depends on internal as well as external factors. The internal factors are mainly connected with the generation of a sufficient volume of saleable surplus and its disposal at competitive prices abroad; the external factors relate to a variety of conditions such as access to foreign markets, advantage or disadvantage of the terms of trade, elasticity of foreign demand for usual export items, effects of tariff and non –tariff barriers and, of course , the continuity of a two-way traffic to prevent lop-sided balance-of –trade.

Evidently, no government would ever think of dealing with all these factors entirely single-handed. What is called for is a division of labour between the government and private business — the former minding bilateral trade negotiations with other nations, advantageous revision of the international institutional arrangements, regulating foreign trade, and appropriate fiscal incentives for export promotion and import –substitution. On the other hand, it will be incumbent upon the businessmen not only to expand production of exportable goods at a level of efficiency that meets international standards of quality and price competition but also to adjust on a regular basis the entire trade apparatus to the exploration of new trade destinations and diversifications of export items. In the case of India it will be seen that the sense of direction the government wanted to develop in matters relating to foreign trade has been generally emulated by the business community.

There has been a visible concern for diversifying India's foreign trade right since the beginning of the Second Five-year Plan, the first having passed off without much headache because of a relatively lower level of import, modest foreign exchange needs for development outlay, and a comfortable balance of payments in the wake of the Korean War boom.[23] Increasing strains on foreign exchange reserve were foreseen, though not in the stupendous proportions they ultimately assumed, in view of the escalation of the level of development expenditure in the second plan. While the makers of the plan stressed the need to augment export earnings through diversification of our exports as the industrial base of the economy expand,[24] the Finance Minister in his 1956-57 budget speech referred to the setting up of Export Promotion Council, Commodity Boards and Export Credit Guarantee Scheme to meet the new situation.[25] At the same time , in its effort to diversify the trade direction, a whole series of new trade agreements were concluded by the government with countries of East Europe, Far East and West Asia.[26]

Though well-timed, this concern for foreign trade did not lead, for quite a long period, to any appreciable improvement in the export performance of the country. As the following table would illustrate, for two successive Five Year Plans and three Annual Plans it failed to remedy the continuing excess of the country's imports over exports.

Responsibility for this deplorable state of affairs lay in no small measure with the public authorities, though there were quite a few attenuating circumstances. In fact the existing inelastic ties of the Indian export market came to be compounded by the unsettling effects of the Chinese invasion (1962) and Indo-Pak hostilities (1965) which made defense import a constant constraint on development while unabated price spiral and continuing industrial recession of the sixties enfeebled the production of exportable surplus. The result was a persistent balance of payments crisis which forced the country to rebuild its trade equations on the basis of a 57.5% devaluation of its currency in 1966. At the level of public policy the snag lay in a deplorable lack of systematic export planning and supplementary fiscal efforts. As an analysis of the National Council of Applied Economic Research[27] points out:

> No attempt was ...made to spell out a coherent export policy or to provide any built –in devices in the plan for creation of exportable surpluses..... everything was left vague, undecided and uncertain 'to be considered from time to time in the light of the actual situation'.....fiscal incentives for export called for new thinking, as it was not in the tradition of the country's fiscal policy; and industry was indifferent to the export trade because it enjoyed the blessings of a sheltered home market.

Table 4.1
India's Foreign Trade 56/57—73/74

Plan Period	Year	Merchandise Value in Crores of Rupees			Exports as % of Imports
		Export	*Import*	*Net*	
Second Plan	1956-57	656.5	1068.3	-411.8	61.5
	57-58	581.7	877.8	-296.1	66.3
	58-59	621.1	945.9	-324.8	65.7
	59-60	633.8	1108.3	-474.5	57.2
	60-61	660.1	1084.5	-424.4	60.9
	Sub-total	3153.2	5084.8	-1931.6	62.0
Third Plan	61-62	668.2	1124.1	-455.9	59.4
	62-63	774.1	1179.5	-405.4	65.6
	63-64	812.8	1342.9	-530.1	60.5
	64-65	803.0	1380.9	-577.9	58.2
	65-66	1155.2	2019.0	-863.8	57.2
	Sub Total	4213.3	7046.4	-2833.1	59.8
Annual	66-67	1209.7	2095.0	-885.3	57.7
Plans	67-68	1320.7	1928.0	-607.3	68.5
	68-69	1376.3	1663.0	-286.7	82.8

Source: United Nations, *The Yearbook of International Trade Statistics*

What however, cannot and should not go unnoticed is that in spite of the ominous portents on the domestic front which arrested the desired outcome, business reaction to the government's line of thinking about trade diversification was remarkably accommodative so far as penetration and nurturing of new markets were concerned.

Three major issues stand out in this connection First, there was the question of the Indo-UK Trade Agreement of 1939. Consequent upon its association with the EFTA countries, the British government requested for release from the preferential tariff arrangement to which Indian goods were entitled in British market under the 1939 agreement. As the government sought the opinion of the FICCI on this question, the latter considered the three available alternatives of (a) flat refusal, (b) insistence on immediate compensation for loss of trade and (c) conditional release subject to subsequent negotiation for compensation "On a balance of considerations" it recommended the third course and advised the government to demand sufficient advance notice form the British government when it would be asking for similar release for entry into the European Common Market.[28] Thus in spite of the adverse repercussions of the proposed change on Indian exports, commercial interests were prepared to face the reality and look for trading channels elsewhere.

This leads one to the second important issue of exploration of new markets abroad. It may be recalled in this connection that as early as April 1960, the FICCI agreed to send a trade delegation to the African continent and came up with the finding that:

> We have substantial trading interests in Egypt and Sudan while the markets of Libya, Tunisia and Morocco require to be developed. Similarly in the East and West African territories we have considerable commercial stake in Ethiopia, Kenya, Uganda, Tanganyika, Rhodesia, Nigeria and Ghana, while considerable effort would be required to develop trade with Mozambique, Belgian Congo, Angola and certain parts of French equatorial Africa.[29]

Nearer home the prospects of trade with the ECAFE region were also investigated. The Indian delegate to the Second Round of Intra Regional Trade Practice talks held at Bangkok form 5 to 14 January 1960 found out that apart from the quality control and competitive price structure, triangular deals with countries receiving foreign aid from western sources and increased import from countries with which India used to have favourable balance of trade (such as Cambodia, Philippines, Thailand and Vietnam) would enhance the country's trading interests.[30]

Obviously, it took some time before these exploratory ventures yielded the desired results of which further discussion will appear in a later chapter. It was clear however, that Indian commercial interests were no longer handicapped by a lack of adventurism and indeed were prepared to make full use of all the new trade channels that public diplomacy was busy opening for them through bilateral agreements.

In fact in certain matters as regional economic cooperation the Indian businessmen appear to have been thinking quite ahead of the government. As early as 1960 the Secretary General of the FICCI, while attending the 17th session of the GATT at Geneva, observed:

> Although I did not imagine that a Common Market comprising developing nations or a payments union of these would be strategically possible, it was quite within the realm of possibility that a well-knit bloc of the remaining member states of the GATT and even those outside it could emerge on the basis of mutually agreeable principles. . .
>
> The reason being:
> The developing nations who are outside these groupings (ref. EEC.EFTA, LAFTA and CMEA) naturally find themselves in a great predicament because, firstly, their bargaining power in the GATT vis-à-vis the member countries of these groups gets greatly reduced and secondly because there is already evidence that group rather than country wise consideration are beginning to prevail in matters where such countries are affected.

These arguments were so convincing that it would not sound far-fetched to suggest a parallel between the well-knit bloc conceived by the FICCI Secretary and the 'Group of 77' which eventually emerged at the forthcoming UNCTAD sessions. In fact, the official Indian delegation did take the necessary initiative at the GATT meeting of October-November 1960 to assemble as many as 19 like-minded countries and confront the world body with a joint memorandum.[31]

The third and perhaps the most knotty issue was the adjustability of private commercial interests with the socialist economies of East Europe whose norms of trade were far from conventional. Nurturing new markets here meant accepting new methods of transaction, mainly consisting in commodity exchange on a planned basis that fosters 'counter-patronage' and self –balancing through rupee payment for all transaction. That the commercial circles in India were initially inclined to try this novel method of trade on rupee payment basis would be evident from the fact that in the decade covering the second and third plan India's total export to all destinations increased by 35 per cent (Rs.604 crores to Rs.813 crores), where-as its exports to the eight East European countries registered an increase by 7.1/2 times (from Rs.21 crores to Rs.157.5 crores).[32] It was soon discovered that these countries are not only "in a position to supply us equipment . . . of quite a lager range and . . . are willing to buy our goods" but there does not seem to be any reservation on their part to trading with private business houses."[33] Within six years from this enthusiastic beginning — a period which saw increasing signs of Soviet political interest in the Indian subcontinent (culminating in the Tashkent mediation, January 1966) and simultaneously of a temporary retreat from the socialist goals of planning by a weak and uncertain regime,[34] the Indian business community started developing serious reservations about the country's trade with East Europe. In a confidential memorandum to Manubhai Shah, then minister of Industries and Commerce, the FICCI President made, *inter alia,* the following disquieting allegations: [35]

(1) "The growth of our trade with East European countries has been at the expense of our export."
(2) "There have been instances where our internationally marketable commodities are exported to other countries at a discount and to our disadvantage"
(3) "The prices paid for machinery imported from East Europe are reported to be higher as compared to imports from other countries, in some cases as high as 25% over the international prices"
(4) "As a result of devaluation of the Rupee, The East European countries safeguarded their interests by providing that prices would be adjusted in proportion to the gold value of the Rupee in the event of any change"

The FICCI President also suggested a few remedial measures, the most striking among them being :
(a) Making export items, other than non-traditional, available only against convertible currency: and
(b) Reverting to multilateral trade system as far as possible.

Without reading into this damaging assessment any ulterior motive which of course should not be surprising in the context of the polarization of forces then taking place in Indian politice,[36] it is possible to see how this untoward reaction of the business community must have placed the public authorities in a fix . In fact the latter were going through trying times marked by an evaporation of western interest in India's economic programmes which were kept in suspended animation through the annual plans, a continuous price-spiral accompanied by industrial recession and widespread unemployment and, of course, a great deal of insecurity on the northern borders since the Chinese explosion of an N-device (October 16,1964) The resultant tensions within the society led to an open split in the Congress party whose ruling half now had no alternative but to adopt a populist stance and a radical rhetoric on most issues — domestic and international . Since this volte face also involved an interesting realignment between the business interests and the government –the latter trying to play the smaller bourgeoisie against the giant monopoly houses it became necessary as well as possible to bypass the apprehensions about bilateral trade with the socialist countries. That the government was satisfied with the finding of its own enquiry into the aforesaid allegations was ciear from the renewal of trade agreement with the USSR and other socialist countries (1966).

While scholarly opinion on the vexed question is far from unanimous[37a] the logic of the situation was quite plain to the decision-makers. As succinctly put in an analysis of the National Council of Applied Economic Research:

> The maintenance of the rupee trade between the socialist countries and India is in any case a shared problem and it is unlikely that with our experience of this trade in the past decade, either we or those countries would risk losing the advantages that have been gradually acquired by allowing a palpable misuse of the trade provision .[37b]

By the same token it did not make much sense to grow nostalgic over multilateral trade in convertible currency with the west : for, sustaining such trade much less improving it had really become a frustrating experience for countries like India in spite of the great diplomatic noise they made at two successive sessions of UNCTAD (1964 AND 1968). Even devaluation which resulted from pressure tactics of the Aid India Consortium did not yield the expected response from western markets. As comparative statistics in the following table show, the old inflexibility continued.

Table 4.2

Directions of India's Trade (for 5 Years following devaluation)

(In million US dollars)

Selected Areas		1967/68	1968/69	1969/70	1970/71	1971/72
Western Europe	Imp.	674.1	589.6	451.3	423.9	656.9
(incl.U.K)	Exp.	488.1	480.2	434.6	459.6	446.3
North America	Imp.	1173.2	1000.0	717.2	764.8	705.6
(incl. U.S.)	Exp.	353.5	314.8	336.3	367.6	315.0
Eastern Europe	Imp.	248.4	303.8	417.8	311.3	274.9
(Inc. USSR)	Exp.	284.8	319.1	350.1	409.6	435.3

Source: *ECAFE-Statistical Yearbook for Asia and the Pacific*

(*UN Publication* No. E/F 77. II F8, 1976)

In fact , it was this inflexibility of trade with developed western market economics that provided the main rationale for diversification of the country's foreign trade. Apart from reducing its dependence on a particular sector of the world market, the country could now use these alternative channels of trade to inject measures of competitiveness among its external buyers and stabilize the precarious terms of trade for many of its traditional export items. Over and above the urgency for expanding India's trade with East European countries stemmed from the new strategy of securing external imports for development through automatic conversion of debt and aid obligations into regular trade flows. This was probably the only commendable course open when the country had little convertible currency at its command to pay for development imports.

Cogent through they were appreciation of these arguments by the commercial circles in the country was not easy to secure. The public authorities, therefore, had to bear the larger brunt of the export drive in the new found markets and even to popularize non-traditional items in old ones. The State Trading Corporation established in 1965 has been playing a very crucial role in this sphere. It has invested or participated in the capital of export oriented enterprises in the country, opened sales promotion offices in foreign capital, fed prospective exporters with the results of its market research and even arranged reshipment finance through government agencies.[38] The government also has been extending liberal grants-in-aid to the export houses for conducting market surveys abroad and also preferential treatment in issuing import license to industries showing good export performance. Short of this leadership which often amounts to parental care not always to the liking of the Merchants' Chamber, use of trade as a method of financing development would have been inconceivable in India and would not have yielded the encouraging results it eventually did.

III. Keeping Foreign Investment at Bay

Public policy regarding foreign investment, like foreign trade, has been the product of national economic reality as perceived by the government and the business community, not necessarily from the same standpoint but generally from a shared concern to lessen the country's dependence on external economic forces.

At the time of independence, members of the Indian business community were still under the hangover of unfulfilled economic nationalism. They readily seized the opportunity of stepping into the areas from which British investors were retiring. The period between 1947 and 1952 witnessed larger scale transfer of ownership or substantial minority holding in Indian hands,[39] In keeping partly with this tendency of self-assertion of local entrepreneurs and partly with the 'Swadeshi' spirit of the nationalist movement , the government announced, as part of its Industrial Policy(April 1948), the intention to "carefully regulate" foreign ventures "in the national interest by ensuring that major interest and effective control should, save in exceptional cases, always be in Indian hands".

Pretty soon it was realized that this hard line was not going to work and called for exceptions that ultimately became the rule. In an interpretive statement that followed Prime Minister Nehru gave existing and intending foreign investors three solemn assurances, viz, no discrimination between foreign and Indian investors; no bar on remittance of profit or repatriation of capital; and full compensation in the event of nationalization which was said to be a remote possibility. To what extent this relaxation was induced by extraneous consideration such as might have arisen during the Commonwealth negotiations in **April 1949** or Nehru's state visit to the USA in **October 1949** is, indeed, difficult to ascertain. To set at rest any such speculation, Nehru rationalized this policy modification in terms of the "need of Indian capital to be supplemented by foreign capital not only because our national saving will not be enough for the rapid development of the country on the scale we wish but also because, in many cases scientific, technical and industrial knowledge and capital equipments can best be secured with foreign capital."[40]

Insofar as this clarification formed the basis of Indian public policy toward foreign investment for years to come, it is necessary to bear in mind its long term implications. To start with, not positive inducement but absence of discriminatory and restrictive regulations was supposed to be the necessary condition for free flow of foreign capital into India, its sufficient condition being provided by the economic opportunities and political climate prevailing in the country. Secondly, as long as foreign investment did not pose any serious threat to the national economic system, it could flourish without any apprehension of being expropriated. Thirdly, the familiar equation of the pre-independence days between foreign investment and economic subjugation was deemed to have been rendered obsolete in the changed context of political independence. Complacency implicit in this reassessment indicated that the early public policies did not give much credence to the view of foreign capital as "a Trojan horse that undermines sovereignty"

The immediate effect of this cautious but optimistic policy stand was noticed in a significant upward trend of foreign investment in the fifties. From the 1953 level of Rs.403.34 crores the total of non-banking foreign investment went up to Rs.506.30 crores. Trade-wise , attraction of foreign capital was relatively higher in productive or marketing ventures in mineral oils, electrical goods, iron and steel products and tea plantations.[41] Besides 'direct investment' as distinguished from portfolio investment accounted for 90% of the operating foreign capital. Also ,as expected, the vacuum created by the earlier flight of British capital which still remains the largest single source of private foreign investments in India came to be filled in by an increasing proportion of American capital rising from Rs.30.06 crores in 1953 to 406.08 crores in 1956.

The trend was slightly reversed during the Second Five Year Plan when the main thrust of development outlay was toward the creation of a heavy industry base and significant expansion of the public sector. This along with the amendment of the property rights under the Constitution gave rise to misgiving in some foreign quarters about the intention of the Indian authorities. Over –reaction in the matter led to the episode of mailed pressure from the World Bank and of American insistence on India's fourth steel plant being placed in the private sector. Nevertheless there was nothing in Nehru's socialist pattern of society that should scare the foreign investors away. As the Prime Minister told the Lok Sabha: [42]

> I am always surprised to hear this proposal being put forward repeatedly: confiscate or expropriate foreign capital. Anything which is more unthinkable, unthought of and nonrealistic I cannot imagine.

In fact the Second Plan, in spite of its heavy weightage in favour of public sector industries, visualized foreign investment to the tune of Rs 100 crores which would take care of a large portion of its foreign exchange component. The concept, really speaking, was one of the seed-sowing of State capitalism in India which, in due course, would be flanked by a subsidiary but nonetheless prosperous private sector. In the ultimate analysis therefore, interests of the private entrepreneurs in India would largely determine the fate of foreign investment. Starting in 1957, the grave foreign exchange crisis into which the Second Five Year Plan ran acted as a catalystic agent to modify the attitude of Indian businessmen toward foreign investment. As the government went ahead with its policies of stringent import control and introduced quantitative restrictions in the hope of import substitution it indirectly prompted Indian capitalists to look for foreign partners who wanted to bring with them capital goods which otherwise it would be difficult to import. The urge behind this partnership idea was provided by the prospects of investments which become brighter with the creation of a whole array of external economics under the development plants.

As businessmen began to overcome their earlier estrangement with foreign capitalists, public policy regarding foreign ventures started changing in favour of an amalgamated investment of local and external capital. This was corroborated by the spate of industrial collaboration agreements receiving government's approval. If between 1943and 1955 such agreements totaled only 447, the figure went up from 1958 to register an annual average of 400 to date. Out of 1951 agreements surveyed by the Reserve Bank of India in 1968, manufacturing accounted for 1006, transport 115, machinery and machine tools 250, metals 107, electrical 162 and chemicals 117. Besides the form of investment was no longer in Indian branches wholly owned by a foreign company but in local subsidiaries and mostly in venture involving minority participations.[43]

Both the governments and the business circles read interesting implications into this development. To the former, it was reassuring to see a large part of foreign capital being invested in enterprises over which Indian industrialists would have substantial controlling interest. With the key industries already sealed off for exclusive management by the public sector, the government had already achieved a good deal of leverage on the private sector and it would be only a matter of technicality to extend the same to the joint ventures. It became so much confident of its controlling power that it allowed even some public sector undertakings to enter into collaboration agreements with foreign concerns.[44] The changed scenario was fully recognized in the following statement of T.T Krishnamachari, Indian Finance Minister: [45]

> I think the stage has come when we should be justified in opening the door even wider for private foreign investment...In the early stages of development there was, I think, every reason for us to take care that vital areas of development were not mortgaged forever to private foreign investment. But now that we have established the vigilant presence of the public sector in most of these vital areas, there is less reason to fear the domination of private foreign investment.

However, it was not the ability to prevent domination of foreign capital but the need to ensure its uninterrupted flow that really brought about moderation of public policy in the sixties. Plagued by persistent imbalance of payments and uncertainty of economic aid, the government had to adopt a softer line towards foreign Investment.

So far as business interests were concerned there were visible signs of disaffection with foreign aid so much so that FICCI memorandum on the Third Five Year Plan recommended 'greater attention to be paid to the inflow of private foreign capital". The FICCI had no reservation about large multinational corporations entering the Indian economies scene for it appreciated that "any significant international investment even when it is restricted to a single manufacturing unit involves such heavy expenditures that only large corporations can undertake it with facility or readiness"[46]

This naturally raised a fundamental question about the future relations between Indian business community and their foreign counterpart. For, sooner or later, it would be incumbent upon the former to choose between the quiescent role of a clientele bourgeoisie and the more assertive role of a self-serving entrepreneur. In either event, public policies would be required to reflect the necessary degree of stringency toward foreign investment. As expected, the Indian business community which had already outgrown the limits of clientele status wanted to protect its independent identity and suggested to the government a six –fold guarantee to the following effect.[47]

(1) Specifying areas where foreign investment will be usually necessary / temporarily necessary/or not necessary at all.
(2) Foreign capital participation normally not to exceed 50%
(3) Provision for progressive Indianisation in cases where majority participation by foreign investment is allowed.
(4) A ceiling of 5% of sales and a time limit of 10 years for technical collaboration to continue
(5) In case of minority foreign holdings, foreign management not to continue beyond ten years.
(6) Freedom of the Indian party to collaboration agreements to export to any destination.

Most of these suggestions found their way to the new industrial licensing policy of the government, announced in the press note of 8 may 1961. There was a clear narrowing of the boundaries within which foreign investment was going to be allowed. An illustrative list of 25 Industries in which foreign capital would ordinarily be welcome was accompanied by a list of the fields in which foreign capital was not required. The latter included: banking, insurance, trading and commercial activities and plantation. Besides, under Section 18A and 18B of the Foreign Exchange Regulation Act (1964) the Reserve bank of India was empowered to deal with cases where a firm controlled by non-residents would act as trade or commercial agents or technical-managerial advisers in India Again foreign equity participation in kind or cash covering the foreign exchange cost of a new industrial undertaking was generally welcome as long as it did not exceed 50% of the total equity, majority ownership being granted only in exceptional cases where: (a) the project is in a high priority industrial field involving a difficult technology not available in the country, (b) the foreign exchange needs exceed 50% of the total equity and could not be provided from other sources if majority equity participation was denied: (c) the foreign collaborator would be exporting a substantial part of the products of the new enterprise: and (d) foreign collaborator agreed to reduce its holding to a minority interest by selling off the balance to the India parties.[48]

It is obvious that these restrictive provisions were addressed to the pursuit of two sets of interest: interest of the nation to ensure the inflow of capital goods and sophisticated technology without drawing upon the country's meager exchange reserve as well as of the local businessmen to enter into new business ventures with a minimum risk but maximum controlling power. However the great snag that crept into this amalgamation of India and foreign capital was that the teaming up occurred mostly between the monopoly houses in the country and giant multi-national corporations with their base in one or more western countries: [49] Of course this alliance need not appear unholy or menacing unless there was a pronounced social bias against it which the government could not entirely overlook except at the peril of its popularity. As it is such a situation arose in the early seventies when widespread social discontent against the government's failure to deliver the good even after two decades of planning led to a sudden radical posture on the part of the ruling elite, epitomized in the populist slogan of "Garibi Hatao" In relation to the corporate sector of the economy, the government was now apparently trying to shift its patronage from the big business house to the medium and small entrepreneurs. [50] Its antimonopoly stance at home coupled with its anti-imperialist rhetoric in foreign affairs presaged some drastic revisions of existing policies toward foreign investment. Announcing its new licensing policy (February. 1973) the government stated without any ambiguity:

> Government's policy will continue to be to encourage competent small and medium entrepreneurs. Such entrepreneurs will be preferred vis-à-vis the lager industrial houses and foreign companies in the setting up of new capacity.

Foreign concerns and subsidiaries if eligible in spite of this preferential treatment for small enterprise will have to be confined to19 core industries deemed to be "of basic , critical and strategic importance " for the growth of the economy and left open for participation of larger industrial houses, resident or non-resident. Foreign investment was not only to remain confined in this core area and operate side by side with indigenous capital: its size would be tailored to suit the official strategies of planned development and honors the stipulation of the MRTPA (Monopolistic and Restrictive Trade Practices ACT 1969).[51] Accordingly, the 1973 Foreign Exchange Regulation Act (FERA) introduced a selective approach to the operation of foreign private capital and imposed a general limit to foreign aquity participation to 40% a level to which existing foreign concerns will have to come down through progressive transfer of their holdings to India hands, a higher percentage of holding being permissible in proportion only to the export potential of the enterprise, e.g., 51% for concerns exporting at least 40% of their product 74% for those exporting at least 60% of their product and so no

Inasmuch as FERA envisaged a total rearrangement of the relative standing of foreign concerns in India, it gave wide ranging powers of the Reserve Bank of India. As many as 1521 applications under Section 28 and 860 applications under Section 29 were submitted to the Bank for clearance of their equity position.[52]

Since a majority of the foreign equity holders agreed to progressive dilution of their holdings, it led to several interesting consequences. To begin with, it set off a veritable race among the country's big business house for control of the areas being vacated by foreign companies since the management of these foreign companies do not favour en block transfer of shares to one or the other of their India partners , it has led to some strained relation between the two.[53]

Secondly, The Reserve Bank of India by virtue of its powers under FERA came to act as the long arm of the government; it immediately ordered 19 companies to discontinue their activities as they were mostly engaged in fields such as real estate, stock brokerage and the like. But the greatest show of political will was found when the newly elected Janata Government cracked down on the two giant U.S based corporations, IBM and Coca-Cola. Both were ordered to wind up their business on the overriding grounds of non-compliance with the requirements for dilution of holdings and refusal to transfer basic technology. In the case of Coca-Cola, overprofiterring in a 'low-priority area' leading to 'runaway growth' was an additional consideration precipitating government action.[54]

The vacuum in each case was soon filled by allowing other international companies to operate in the area in close collaboration respectively with two governments undertakings: the Computer Maintenance Corporation of India and the Central Food Technological Research Institute.

Although political temper rose high in the Indian parliament over these two cases, it did not lead to any diplomatic recrimination between the host and home governments.[56] After all, these concerns were not nationalized but were told to wind up their business. Barring the case of the foreign oil companies (74% of whose shares were taken over by the government in 1974), the authorities so far do not appear to have taken any punitive measures against any foreign company. However, the variety of obnoxious trade practices of which the MNC's are so frequently being accused in and outside the Parliament[55] cannot continue long without provoking serious reaction on the part of government. Especially, it remains to be seen how far and how long the government could remain blind to the excessive outflow of foreign exchange by way of super profits, high divedends, inflated head office expenses and so on.[57]

The government's arsenal in regulatory multinational enterprise in India consists up till now of

(a) Pre-registration scrutiny of undertaking given by the foreign investor regarding R and D expenditure, export obligation, sharing and transfer of technology, etc at the level of Foreign Investment Board(Set up in 1968);
(b) Restricting the operation of foreign capital in nationally defined priority areas and;
(c) Post-registration fade out arrangements through dilution of holdings.
(d) In the main, these methods provide advance safe guards against undue penetration of foreign capital into the vital areas of the country's economy. Besides, since joint ventures constitute the most preferred form for foreign capital to be employed in Indian business and since the bulk of these ventures now involve technical collaboration rather than financial participation,[58] the necessary vigilance on foreign capital can be easily shared between public

authorities and local private business. Finally, there is a whole chain of scrutinizing agencies through which the compulsory Annual Returns from undertakings with foreign collaboration must be cleared[59] for the agreements to survive their initial period of validity.

Considering all these aspects it may be concluded that cautious optimism and advance programming on the part of the government together with a vigilant local bourgeoisie have so far enabled the country to keep foreign investment at bay while using it to the fullest extent for economic development. In fact in these days when multinational business is increasingly being identified as the latest and the most formidable expression of neo-imperialism it is no mean achievement to have channeled foreign investment into selected fields where technological or critical production gap exists and to have tried to cut it down to minority position as a matter of general routine. The confidence that grew in the course of the last three decades of managing foreign investment in India found full expression in Industrial Policy(December 23,1977) which points out *inter alia* that foreign investment and acquisition of technology necessary for India's industrial development would be only on such terms as are determined by the Government to be in the national interest.[60] The situation obtaining today offers an instructive commentary on how the balance of power between foreign investors and host government can be[61] steadily tilted in favour of the latter. From the stronger bargaining position it now enjoys, the government can now intervene in areas which were once the exclusive province of the foreigner e.g choice of foreign consultants, extent of royalty payment, employment of nationals in supervisory positions and earmarking the proportion of produces that should be marketed abroad.

That these counter-dependency measures need not scare away prospective investors but can make them enter into a game of mutual accommodation is corroborated by the unmistakable growth of foreign business investments in India over time. In fact a reversal of this trend will mean anything but sound economics, when a comparative stock is taken of the profitability position of foreign concerns in India.

Table 4.3

Profitability Position of Companies in India

Gross Profits as Percentage of Total Capital Employed (in per cent)

Year	Subsidiaries	Minority Companies	Purely technical Collaboration Companies
	1	2	3
1964-65	16.8	9.5	12.0
1965-66	15.7	9.5	11.7
1966-67	15.2	8.6	10.9
1967-68	14.5	8.3	9.0
1968-69	15.8	8.4	9.4
1969-70	17.2	9.6	9.8
Average for 1964-70	15.9	9.0	10.5
Average for 1960-64	15.5	8.5	11.8

Source: RBI Survey Report on Foreign Collaboration in Indian Industry 1974.

Given this comfortable rate of return, there is little reason to suppose that foreign investors want to fight shy of the Indian economy and when they do, the reason must be attributed to an implacable contradiction between the objectives of natural development and the self-serving interests of the foreign capitalist.

References

1. The main directions of this process have been discussed in Michael H Best and William E. Connally, *The Politicized Economy*, pp 22-28, D.C.Heath, Lexington Mass. 1976
2. FICCI, *Correspondence & Relevant Documents* 1942-43, vol II, P285.
3. Ibid p 294.
4. Ibid p 295
5. V.S. Vartikar, *Commercial Policy and Economic Developments in India*, chap 6 Praegar, New York, 1969; also; Yogendra Prasad Verma, *Growth of Protectionism in India*, chap 4,5 S chand, New Delhi, 1974.
6. Nehru's speeches, 1946-49 pp 142-43.
7. GOI, Industrial Policy Resolution (April 30,1956), Second Five Year Plan,pp 43-50
8. Ajit Ray, *Sharers in India's State and Society, A Marxist Approach*, p141,Orient Longman, Bombay,1975
9. Assistance sanctioned by these financing institutions to the corporate sector of India's economy amount to year wise"
   1972...............342.7 crores

1973...............325.9 crores
1974...............446.7 crores
1975...............562.8 crores
Source: *Statistical Outline of India* 1976 Tata Services Ltd 1976, p 99

10. First officially expressed in Nehru's landmark speech to the National Development Council on November 9, 1954 and at Avadi session Congress Resolution on Socialistic Pattern of Society (January 1955)
11. H.V.R Iengèr, *Buisness and Planned Economy* ,pp 165-168, Vora, Bombay, 1988; Babubhai M Chinani, *India's March to Democratic Socialism*,pp 5-11, Brihad Bharatiya Samaj, Bombay,1972
12. The public-private sectors controversy took serious proportions in the early sixties when Chinese invasion and the bleak performance of the Five Year Plans led to a demand by the business sector for a reversal of the role of the two sectors see Frankel, op.cit.ch vi
13. The controversy continued unabated till the turning of the corner by the public undertakings with a net profit of Rs 17.7 crores in 1972-73
14. See D.O. communications of FICCI Presidents R.B.Amin to G.S.Pathak. Union Law Minister, dated May 7, 1965, *FICCI Documents and Correspondence 1966*, p145
15. FICCI President S.S Kanoria's warning statement, *FICCI Fortnightly Review*, p4, August 16, 1971.
16. The proposed means of control are mainly these: exercise of voting rights in respect of shares held by or pledged with financial institutions including nationalized banks conversion of loans into equity holding at the option of the financial institutions, and appointment of government nominee on the Board of Directors of private companies.
17. (a) Letter of FICCI President A.M.M. Chettiar to Prime Minister Nehru, 18 April 1960, FICCI Documents and Correspondence 1961,p 179
17. (b) FIICI, *Third Five Year Plan. A tentative outline*
17. (c) FICCI *Documents and Correspondence*, op.cit p255
18. The concept of Joint Sector involves State-Private collaborative ventures.
19. See n.9; also Bhupesh Gupta, *25 Years of Independence*,CPI Freedom Jubilee Series No1, p16 New Delhi, August,1972
20. Girish Misra, *Public Sector in India's Economy*, pp 39-40, CPI Publication no 4, New Delhi,1975
21. Bhabatosh Datta, *Private Sector and the National Planning Process*, in R.C Dutt and R.K Nigam(ed) *Towards Commanding Heights*, SCOP, New Delhi,1975, pp268-269. Telling revelation of this dependence was also admitted by FICCI report on Industrial Recession (mimeograph) pp 2-6, New Delhi,1966
22. See *FICCI Documents and Correspondence* 1961, pp 30-49, 146-48,168-76 and 1966 pp 7-8, 10-34
23. *RBI Report on Currency and Finance* 1955-56 p 70
24. *Second Five Year Plan, A Draft Outline*, p33
25. *Lok Sabha Debates*, February 29, 1956, vol1 No12, col 1185.
26. *Journal of Industry and Trade*, April 1957, p704
27. NCAER, *Export Strategy for India*, New Delhi, 1969, p7
28. *FICCI Documents and Correspondence* 1961 pp122-23
29. ibid pp12021
30. Report of S.R Biswas, Secretary, Bengal Chamber of Commerce to FICCI.
31. *FICCI Documents and Correspondence* 1961 pp 152 and 526

32. NCAER, OP.CIT. PP 101.2
33. *FICCI Documents and Correspondence* 1961 pp 533
34. Frankel, op, cit. chap VII
35. *FICCI Documents and Correspondence* 1961 pp 59-67
36. The polarization was sharpened by the reaction of right wing forces within and outside the Congress Party to the prospect of progressive social control of the more prosperous elements in the society and the inevitability of a pro-Soviet tilt of the government in international affairs.
37. (a) Two contrasting analyses are found in Deepak Nayyar, *India's Trade with Socialist Countries* in Nayyar (ed) *Economic Relations between the Socialist Countries and the Third World,* pp 105-141 and R.Mukherjee, *Economics of Soviet Trade and Aid,* pp 55-100, Subarnarekha, Calcutta, 1978.
37. (b) op. cit. p 105
38. K.R Gupta, *Working of State Trading Corporation in India* pp 142-50, S.Chand & Co., *State Trading Corporation in Developing Countries,*pp 166-67, Rotterdam University Press, 1969
39. 64 out of 66 countries bought over by Indians was British owned. See K.M Kurian, *Impacts of Foreign Capital on Indian Economy,* Delhi, 1966,l p71.
40. CAD, Vol IV, I.col 2385.
41. *RBI Bulletin* September 1958; also, *RBI Survey of India's Foreign Liabilities and Assets,* Bombay 1958.
42. *Lok Sabha Debates* 11 April 1955, pt ii, Vol III no 37, col4840-41. See also T.T Krishhnamachari's statement to the Associated Chambers of Commerce, *The Hindu,* and December 13, 1955
43. RBI, *Foreign Collaboration in Indian Industries: Survey Report,* pp4 and 102, Bombay,1968.
44. Out of 41 Government Companies surveyed by the RBI in its Second Survey Report,39 had enterd into 163 technical collaborations p 85. Report 1974.
45. T.T. Krishnamachari speech cit. Hazari *Foreign Collaboration,* infra.
46. FICCI, *Third Five Year Plan,* op.cit p.13
47. FICCI *Documents and Correspondence* 1966 PP317-319
48. R.K Hazari, Foreign Collaboration, University of Bombay, 1967.
49. GOI Department of Company Affairs, *Company News and Notes Fortnightly,* Delhi January 1,1969.
50. Vide the social objectives of the Fifth Plan which obtained a mandatory character under the 20 point programme of Mrs. Gandhi.
51. GOI Ministry of Industrial Development, *Report,* Appendix IV, pp 139-45, New Delhi 1973
52. C. Subramanian in Lok Sabha August 20, 1976, LXII col 62.
53. *Far Eastern Review,* vol 99, No13, March 31, 1978, P47. Hongkong
54. Described by George Fernandes Industries Minister, as 'a classic example of how a multinational corporation...was stifling weaker indigenous industry....' Ibid
55. Robert Goheen, US Ambassador to India had to assure that the Coca-cola controversy did not vitiate Indo-US relations.
56. See O.P Bhatia, *The Role of Multinationals in India,* about the Catalogue of complaints, *Asian Labour,* no 116, pp 11-13, February, 1975
57. As the RBI survey shows 36 top foreign firms repatriated Rs. 1089.7 million out of a total remittance of Rs 2623 million during 1968-71.

58. This will appear from the R.B.I Survey, ibid
59. See Appendix II & IV , of GOI, Director General of Technical Development *Report on Foreign Collaborations*, New Delhi, 1974
60. *Annual Report of the Ministry of Industry* 1977-78, pp 277-78
61. The implication of course is not that the outcome is to be expected in all circumstances. Chile providing a sad exception.

5
The Perspective of Inter-Developing Economics

One of the enduring contributions of India's policy of non-alignment toward strengthening her world position was the opportunity it offered for developing closer ties with other less developed regions of the world. From the viewpoint of political economy, it enabled the country's leadership to appreciate the common problems of development confronting the peoples in these areas, which in the nature of things, also demanded common endeavour for their satisfactory solution. Small wonder, therefore, India Has been found sailing in the same boat with an increasing number of developing nations in their journey towards a more equitable international economic order. While, politically, non-alignment offered most of these developing nations a viable method of preserving an area of peace away from great power rivalry and conducive to national economic reconstruction, the need for economic cooperation among them was heightened by the inadequacy and iniquities of their veritcal relationship with the industrially advanced countries in the west.

As the basic antagonism between the developing and the developed countries bacame explicit through multilateral economic diplomacy beginning with the Bretton Woods and Havana Conferences of the forties and continuing with greater vigour during the development decades of the sixties and seventies, two pressing needs arose for the developing countries in their international dealings. One was the creation of a common platform from which to negotiate a better deal with the developed countries; the other was the progressive inter-weaving of development efforts. The first was, and still is, relevant to the demand of the developing countries for structural and institutional changes in international economic transactions to which the advanced countries evince a kind of habitual resistance. The second has only lately become significant with the discovery of a new comparative advantage that inheres in the development differential obtaining between the developing countries themselves. Delay in this discovery was partly due to the 'metropolitan obsession' of most of these countries recovering from a long spell of colonialism and mostly due to the gestation period involved in exploiting the national economic potential. The latter alone could bring into bolder relief the main contours of economic growth which warranted conscious complementing of development efforts by the countries concerned, in order to avoid unnecessary duplication in areas where mutual exchange is more advantageous and also to minimise the dependency effects of an asymmetric economic linkage with industrially advanced nations.

India, because of its early involvement in economic planning and persistent efforts at fending off great power hegemony, has naturally taken great interest in this search for complementarities among developing countries. A review of her role in building up a common front of the developing countries and the extent of her commitment to the task of 'inter-developing' should provide a new dimension to the understanding of the political economy of her foreign policy.

I. Common Front of the Developing Countries

Ever since her independence India has been consistently trying to make the development of nations a matter of international concern. In his very first appearance before the UN General Assembly, Nehru wanted the world body to deemphasise its political pre-occupations and take a serious look at the economic problems that ultimately endangered peace. At a time when few took the Assembly to be the proper forum to raise such questions, Nehru made the trend-setting observation.

> "It is a strange thing, when the world lacks so many things food and other necessities in many parts of the world.... the attention of this Assembly of Nations is concentrated only on a number of political problems... I wonder if it would be possible for this Assembly to take a holiday for a while from some of the acute political problems which face it, and allow men's minds to settle down and look at the vital and urgent economic problems."

Earlier at Bretton Woods (1944) and Havana (1947-48) India had argued against the perpetuations of the existing International division of labour and vigorously advocated incorporation of economic development of backward countries in the Fund-Bank framework. Being no party to the US Lend-Lease Agreement and expecting the release of a large reserve of sterling balances from U.K. after the World War II, she had a relatively strong negotiating position to take this rather non-conformist stance. Precious little, however, was done in these conferences for alleviation of the problem of underdevelopment the main reason being the dominance of the Western view about post-war economic restoration.

The next important occasion of India to reopen the matter arose when the twelfth session of the UN General Assembly devoted its attention to the question of a special UN Development Fund. The Indian delegation along with ten other representing Argentina, Ceylon, Egypt, Greece, Indonesia, Mexico, the Netherlands, Venezuela and Yugoslavia submitted a draft resolution on the proposed Fund (SUNFED) in order to counteract American attempt to dilute its purpose by making it a mere extension of the existing programme of technical assistance (EPTA). In the welter of controversy that followed India struggled hard to keep alive the idea of an internationally controlled capital development fund though in the end she had to settle for a compromise Special Projects Fund because of the wavering attitude of some of the co-sponsors of her resolution.[2] It was not until the first UN Development Decade that anything substantial emerged in respect of the Indian proposal. At the twenty-first session of the General Assembly India could clinch the issue by successfully launching a resolution, co-sponsored by forty other delegations, which "decide (d) to bring into operation the United Nations Capital Development Fund as an organ of the General Assembly, which shall function as an autonomous organization within the United Nation".[3] Resistance of the developed countries now turned into a refusal to participate in the Pledging Conference which initially attracted some $1.29 million pledge of contribution from 25 countries and subsequently rose to $4.4 million upto June 1971, when erstwhile recalcitrant contributors also came within its purview.[4]

The question of development finance assumed greater urgency in the sixties with the onset of the Development Decade and the eventual international recognition of the corelation between trade and development.[5] The 1961 Belgrade Conference of Non-aligned countries had already focussed attention on the economic status of third world countries.[6] The phillip was carried over to the economic conference of these countries in Cairo (1962) and largely conditioned the diplomatic alignment at the ensuing UNCTAD (1964). Bilateral relationship between an economically weak and a strong country being basically an unequal relationship it was found necessary to adopt joint positions and multilateral approaches in international economic negotiations. This was the spirit behind the formation of the Croup of 77. As aptly pointed out in an analysis of UNCTAD diplomacy.[7]

> Although the number of new and rapidly developing nations which had joined the United Nations during the last few years occupy a substantial portion of the earth, the balance of power had not shifted... The Conference seemed to offer an opportunity to change this state of affairs; and, indeed, when at the end of the conference seventy seven underdeveloped nations submitted a joint declaration, a landmark was set.

Even during the deliberations in the committees and the plenary sessions it was remarkable how the developing nations acted in unison. "Although each delegation spoke for its own government and its own economy, the indication of certain kinship among nations became discernible. As could be expected, there were similarities in the approach of developing countries on the one hand and of industrialized countries on the other."[8]

Considering the need to further consolidate this new found solidarity India suggested to the thirty one members from Africa, Asia and Latin America on the Board of Trade and Development that a meeting of the Group of 77 should be convened to prepare their strategy for the Second UNCTAD. The ministerial meeting of the Group was held in Algiers in October 1967, which resulted in the famous Algiers Charter containing the negotiating premises for the developing countries. Reporting on the impact it created on the second UNCTAD held in New Delhi (February-March 1968), Dinesh Singh, Minister of Commerce, told the Lok Sabha that only five out of the twenty commodities listed in the Algiers Charter figured in the commodities agreement and the much publicised Generalised Non-discriminatory, Non-reciprocal Preferential system was agreed upon only in principle. No definite commitment from the developed countries regarding tariff liberalisation and removal of non-tariff barriers was available. However the terms od DAC aid held out prospects of progressive softening in terms of aid, rescheduling of debt servicing and refinancing in appropriate cases. While the net outcome of the confernece was far from encouraging (an assessment shared also by the Secretary General, Raul Prebisch),[9] India had reasons to be gratified with the "close and concerted working of the group of developing countries" which now were 90 in number and had scored at least one political victory in getting racist South Africa expelled from the UNCTAD.[10]

Of course, the group system had the mixed result, on the one had, of formulating well-defined objectives for joint action and, on the other, of compelling an agreement on the lowest common denominator of demands pressed by the developing countries. It is true that the latter was hardly acceptable to the more radical members of the Group of 77 like Ghana. Algeria and Burma. But India decided to play an evidently realistic role in UNCTAD II for a couple of compelling reasons. First, the country's increasing indebtedness to the Western donor nations made her depend on some concessions expected from them in respect of debt service relief. Secondly, she was particularly anxious to have some concrete and positive decisions on the Generalised System of Preferences which she badly needed to make good the impending loss of preferential trade with Britain then only a few steps away from entry into the EEC. Thirdly, and this was not inconsequential, she did not want the differences within the Group of 77 to assume any serious proportion that would give the developed countries of the West an opportunity to out wit the developing countries.

The role of India in the next UNCTAD session at Santiago (April-May 1972) was less diffident. This time greater caution was taken in preparing the joint position paper (the Lima Charter) which put a brake on split in the ranks of the developing nations; in fact, its acceptance by China, a new addition to UNCTAD membership, enhanced its weight. On her own part, India, now wiser by the lessons of the Bangladesh crisis, set less store by the vagaries of foreign assistance and disseminated her view of economic self-reliance which came to be shared by a large number of the developing countries attending the Santiago session. The Indian delegation at Santiago argued vigorously for a link between the SDR (Special Drawing Rights) proposed to be created as new international liquidity by the IMF and the funds at the disposal of the International Development Association for soft-loan disbursement to developing countries. It also presented a cogent case for regulation of the oligopolistic practice of the shipping interests belonging to the developed countries securing a Conference reference of the whole matter to the UN General Assembly for necessary steps to formulate an international shipping code.

Connected with expansion and stabilization of international trade in favour of the developing countries was the vital question of reform of the international monetary system. This assumed great urgency since the middle of 1971 when international exchange market started facing uncertainty about the role of US dollar as a reserve currency. As the dollar holdings of certain European and Asian countries swelled in the wake of persistent deficit in the US balance of payments, the American government suspended in August 1971 the convertibility of dollar into gold. This gave added impetus to the movement already afoot since 1968 for speedy conversion of the dollar standard into a system in which a neutral reserve asset like the SDR would become the principal asset of the system. In this respect India had all along been insisting that any vital decision about the future of the world monetary system should no longer remain the exclusive concern of a limited group of countries controlling the IMF. It was largely as a result of this protest being voiced simultaneously by a number of other developing countries that the IMF agreed to set up in September 1972 the committee of 20 to advise the IMF Board of Governors on international monetary reforms.

At the Nairobi meeting of the Committee of 20 India submitted a six-fold proposal the essence of which lay in providing a stable through adjustable par value system with SDR acting as the principal international liquidity the accumulation of which should be used to facilitate transfer of real resources for the development programmes of backward countries.[12] Opportunity was also taken to highlight these points and obtain support of the Commonwealth countries at the Ottawa Conference of the Commonwealth Heads of Government on Trade, Tariff and Monetary Matters.[13] While reiterating India's stand on the question of international monetary reforms, Y.B. Chavan, the Union Finance Minister told the IMF-IBRD members at the Annual Meeting[14] held in Nairobi (September 1973):

> ...the one solid impression I am left with is that the aspirations of the developing countries can be fully met only if there is adequate political will and vision on the part of the developed countries.

Since there was nothing automatic about this change of heart taking place in the developed world, the Indian Finance Minister further reminded:

> The new Fund will be structured in a manner that will accord to the developing countries the role which they deserve by virtue of their numbers and size in the decision-making process of the Fund...Any attempt at reform of the international monetary system must ensure that the orgainsiation builds ups its structure in the interest of the world community rather than in the interest of any limited group of members, however big or important these might be.

Of equal importance as finance is another issue, namely food supply which attracted serious international attention in the seventies and gave birth to the idea of a World Food Council. India being one of the countries hard hit frequently by crop failure due to drought, flood and other natural calamities took special interest to make an international issue of the food crisis. Assuring full support to the imaginative programme presented by the FAO Director-General Dr A.H. Boerma at the Seventh General Conference of the Orgainsiation in Rome (November 1973), the Indian Minister of Agriculture, Fakhruddin Ali Ahmed proposed an action-oriented approach involving a food buffer against future shortfall in production, a fertilizer buffer to optimize production in irrigated areas, a crop research programme not only to breed high-yield varieties but also to devise suitable crop weather models, increased availability of power supply for agriculture and, above all, a curb on over-consumption where it was taking place. To quote Ahmed:

> The space ship earth is unfortunately divided into two compartments and those living in the first class compartment are consuming a disproportionate part of the available sources of food and energy. For the vast majority squeezed in the small second class compartment, life is becoming increasingly miserable and hard ...if the compartment of the poor collapses due to excessive pressure, the whole space ship will crash.[15]

In dealing with emergent problems of international economic relations, India was thus not only trying to press for changes that would be conducive to her own interests but also speak for the entire group of developing nations with whom she found it necessary to maintain a common front.

II. Non-alignment and Economic Cooperation

This common front strategy intended to reinforce her bargaining power with the developed nations is followed by India with greater intensity within the more familiar confines of the non-aligned movement. One interesting consequence of this is the new direction in which the movement is now being channeled, showing a discernible shift of interest from political to economic matters. The process which began at the Cairo Conference (October 1964) when Prime Minister Shastri urged that the developing nations must "help each other even before we seek assistance from outside"[16] assumed special significance at the Lusaka Conference (September 1970). Prime Minister Indira Gandhi referred to the "areas of cooperation in many fields of development" in the exploration of which "India would be glad to play her modest part."[17] The Lusaka Conference adopted a Programme of Action which envisaged specific projects for which import requirements should be met from the developing countries and recommended mutual support of industrial expansion and increased flow of trade among the member countries. Details of the programme came up for discussion at the 17-nation Coordinating Bureau of non-aligned countries at Algiers (May-June 1976). The comprehensiveness of the Programme can be guessed from the following report of the Indian Ministry of External Affairs;[18]

> This programme, while covering old and familiar fields of cooperation, namely, trade, industrailisation, science, technology, monetary and financial cooperation, raw materials, etc. contained new additional sections on food and agriculture, fisheries, transport, telecommunications, insurance, public enterprises, health, technical cooperation and consultancy services, employment and human research and information system and tourism.

That these projects were going to have necessary financial backing was clear from the plan of action announced at the Lima conference (August 1975) which established a solidarity fund for the economic and social development of the non-aligned countries with equal subscription for membership fixed at 500,000 SDR. Besides, a group of experts has been working on the establishment of a Special Fund for financing buffer stocks of raw materials and primary products.[19]

So far as India's own contribution is concerned, it flows along three distinet channels: transfer and economic assistance, industrial cooperation through international agencies and setting up of joint industrial ventures abroad.

Transfer of state capital is the principal Indian way of extending economic aid to other developing countries. Though the absolute figures of Indian aid look small compared to aid flowing from other donors, the fact that India, in spite of herself being dependent on foreign assistance for her economic development, has nonetheless managed to apportion a part of her investible resources for various projects in a number of other developing countries. Up till now, the recipients in this category and the amount of aid flow are respectively: Nepal–around a billion Rupees between 1950 and 1974; Sri Lanka–loans worth 37 crores between 1961 and 1975; Indonesia–Rupee credit of 10 crores; Bangladesh–over 2.2 billion Rupees as grants-in-aid and credit; Burma–loan of Rupees 20 crores; and Bhutan–grants-in-aid of Rupees 38 crores. In addition, substantial assistance of technical nature is accorded through the Colombo Plan, which amounted to Rupees 5.8 crores by 1974. These funds are partly used for deputing Indian specialists to assist and advise the recipient countries in such matters as irrigation, fisheries development, small scale industries, railways, shipping and aviation, and even organising statistical services.[20] (See Appendix)

In respect of industrial cooperation through international agencies India has been playing an important role in the UNIDO and UNDP. She was elected Chairman of the Ad hoc committee formed under General Assembly recommendation in Resolution 2823 (XXVI) to suggest the long-range strategy to be followed by these agencies in respect of appraisal and approval of industrial projects in developing countries. She also pledged a sum of $50,000 in non-convertible rupees for UNIDO's operational programmes. In addition to supplying Indian expertise to different countries as and when requested by the UNIDO, she is also taking substantial interest in the modalities of technology transfer in different spheres. The subsidiaries of ECAFE such as Asian Industrial Development Council (AIDC) also benefit from the association of Indian experts.[21]

But the most important aspect of India's economic interaction with the developing countries relates to the setting up of joint industrial ventures abroad both by public sector units and by private investors. The main impetus for this development arose out of the relevance of the Indian experience in development planning to many newly independent countries of Asia and Africa which not only shared common economic problems with India but, comparatively speaking, where late starters in the march towards economic development. Earlier import of western technology by Indian entrepreneurs and their subsequent assimilation and modification made Indian technology more suited to the conditions of the developing countries where industrial ventures, at least in the formative stage, have necessarily to be less capital intensive and more labour-dependent. Indian technology also offers distinct price advantage inasmuch as the overall cost of importing technology from the industrially advanced countries often appears to be prohibitive. The success of Indian industries in the bid for international tenders for the supply of railway wagons, locomotive engines and coaches, industrial part, bicycles, sewing machines, electric fans and so on in a number of Asian and African countries is illustrative of this cost differential. Of course, familiarity with the local set up on the part of Indian business communities who have settled in many of the countries together with the incentives provided by the Indian government through modest but effective technical assistance as well as training facilities at Indian institutions also contribute to the continuing expansion of Indian joint ventures abroad.

As records show, positive government interest in this matter did not develop till the mid-sixties, conservation of foreign exchange being the main headache which discouraged export of Indian capital for overseas investment. In the wake of liberal economic policies, visible since August 1964, the government allowed Indian investment in equities abroad, the subscription of share capital being obtained through supply of machinery and equipments. Subsequently, as trade showed the path to investment, the industrial goodwill delegation sponsored by the Federation of Indian Chambers of Commerce (September-October 1964) came back from a tour of African countries with the findings that[22]

> in her own interest India can no longer rely on conventional method of trading and the newer techniques demand that we must actually participate in setting up joint industrial ventures in as large a measure as possible.

Joint venture instead of direct investment in subsidiaries was preferred because this "will not provoke the same resentment and antagonism that purely Indian business establishments run by domiciled Indian might tend to do."[23] In permitting Indian participation in the proposed joint ventures, authorities in India generally follow a few precautionary considerations. For instance, it allows only minority participation upto 49% of the foreign equity exceptions being made only in those cases where the host government is agreeable to higher Indian holdings. Besides, they make sure that dividends and profits accruing from these investments are, for the most part, ploughed back in the country of investment. The Ministry of Industrial Development has a full fledged joint venture cell which disseminates information and gives incentive in order to channel Indian investment into prospective areas; foreign exchange upto 10 % of the Indian share capital is also provided by the government to help meet the promotional expenses of a new venture.

On analysis it would appear that most of these ventures are engaged in the production of durable consumer goods and intermediate capital goods; in terms of area orientation they are mostly concentrated in the countries belonging to West Asia, Southeast Asia and Africa. In recent times public sector units such as the Fertiliser Corporation of India, State Trading Corporation of India, Hindustan Machine Tools and Hindustan Telephones have come to play a role sufficient to match the activities of private business interst in the sphere of foreign investment. Interestingly, large industrial houses of the Birlas, Tatas, Kirloskar, Sarabhai and the like account for more than one-third of these investments, the total (including actual and proposed till 1972) is estimated at Rupees 20 crores.[24]

The overall effects of these multifarious activities on the part of the government in international forums aided by trade and investment efforts have been quite favourable in ordering the country's foreign relations. As the Minister of State for External Affairs, Surendar Pal Singh, stated while replying to the Lok Sabha Debates on budget demands:[25]

> We are giving more importance to the economic aspect of our foreign policy. It is our firm belief that... there is now a growing awareness among the countries of Asia and Africa about the competence and ability of this country to be a provider of technical knowhow and expertise ....in spite of our difficulties at home, despite our own limitations, we have done everything possible to share our experience, our resources with a large number of countries, and we have done everything possible to help them in their difficult task of economic and industrial development. I must say that this approach to our foreign policy has already paid some very handsome dividends inasmuch as it has greatly increased the goodwill, friendship and trade between ourselves and a large number of countries in Africa and Asia.

III. Role of Joint Commissions in Bilateral Economic Cooperation

No survey of India's involvement in an inter-developing system with other similarly placed countries will be complete without taking a look at the operations of the Joint Commissions through which the country's bilateral economic relations are being coordinated. This institutional innovation to which a passing reference has been made in Chapter III deserves a detailed treatment in the context of the interweaving of economic growth to which the Indian policy makers are devoting increasing attention.

Although the Joint Commissions in their present from have only lately been receiving considerable attention in public economic diplomacy, the basic idea behind them was not unknown to earlier efforts to organise bilateral economic transactions. Thus in 1959, after a trade delegation under K.B. Lall, then Additional Secretary, Ministry of Commerce and Industry, visited a number of West European capitals, the delegation recommended the establishment of joint commissions in Italy, Switzerland, France, Belgium and Germany "with a view to ensuring effective implementation of the agreements." The commissions, composed of government representatives at the commercial counsellor or secretary level, were expected to "meet at periodical intervals and seek to evolve solutions to difficulties that are hampering trade between the countries."[26] Little thought was given at this point about the wisdom and possibility of utilisation of these commissions beyond the settlement of ordinary trade difficulties so that they could act as regular channels of economic diplomacy. One possible explanation seems to be that the orgaisational pattern of the Indian Ministry of External Affairs was rather archaic with practically no room for a regular cell to deal with the economic aspects of foreign policy or for any meaningful collaboration with the other ministries dealing with economic matters. Changes in the direction were visible only in the mid-sixties when a Policy Planning and Review Committee (as envisaged by the Pillai committee of 1965) was required to "evaluate the adequacy of the current policies" in the light of.... political economic and security aspects of a question."[27] However, the requisite dovetailing of either the agencies or the polices involved was not forthcoming until early seventies when foreign policy goals appeared incapable of achievement without the support of complementary economic relations with other nations.

The Economic Division of the Ministry of External Affairs which was set up in the sixties to promote joint thinking among the various allied ministries was given a new dimension of activities as the industrial economy of the country was maturing to reach the stage where it would need an integrated strategy of development with other developing countries offering good prospects for trade and investment for the Indian entrepreneurs. This required a three-fold programme of action:

Promotion of closer external economic and commercial relations on the basis of bilateral agreements.

Expansion of the technical assistance programme (ITEC) in an attempt to propagate Indian technology in other developing countries.

1. Mutual support for economic cooperation at the regional and multilateral level.

The Joint Commissions are supposed to provide the necessary institutional framework within which these activities could be coordinated and which would provide a forum for discussing the strategies to be adopted at multilateral economic negotiations.[28] Starting with the Indo-Czech Joint Committee in 1966, Joint Commissions have now been established between India on the one hand and a large number of countries belonging to Western market economies, Centrally Planned economies of East Europe and the developing continents of Asia and Africa. As of 1977, the following countries have been using Joint Commissions in their economic and commercial dealings with India:

Asia	Afghanistan	(operative since 1969)
	Iran	(........................ 1969)
	Iraq	(........................ 1973)
	Sri Lanka	(........................ 1968)
	United Arab Emirate	(........................ 1975)
	Saudi Arabia (preliminaries settled in 1975)	
Africa	Nigeria	(operative since 1977)
	Sudan	(........................ 1973)
	Tanzania	(........................ 1976)
Latin America	Guyana	(........................ 1978)
North America	USA	(........................ 1974)
West Europe	France	at the level of Joint Committee or groups
	Belgium	
	Netherlands	
	U.K.	
East Europe	Czechosilovakia	(operative since 1966)
	Poland	(........................ 1972)
	USSR	(........................ 1972)
	Bulgaria	(........................ 1973)
	Hungary	(........................ 1973)
	Rumania	(........................ 1974)
	GDR	(........................ 1975)

As more of these Joint Commissions come into being either through fresh initiative or by upgrading the existing committees or consultative groups, India would be increasingly surrounded by a network of economic cooperations. This would not only give her a unique opportunity of discovering and developing complementarities with other economics and of using such complementarities for her own economic development, but is likely in course of time to enable her to place political relations with these countries on a more stable footing than has been possible under the conventional methods of diplomacy.

The Joint Commissions which have been described as 'clearing houses to strengthen economic and technical cooperation' [29] have been found to serve a useful purpose by allowing isolated bilateral economic agreements and aspects of economic relations with a country to be reviewed and assessed periodically against the totality of economic and political relations that is sought to be developed with it. This also ensures that additional fields of cooperation are explored in keeping with the changing needs of industrial and commercial development of the countries concerned. Since these Commissions generally meet annually and delegations are led at the ministerial level, it can be reasonably expected that the deliberations and decisions of these meetings would provide a serious insight into the problems and prospects of inter-developing. It would also clarify the global perspective of the economic relations between nations insofar as India as the common link between the developing and developed countries included in these Joint Commissions could very well supplement and influence the individual outlook of these countries in regard to mutual cooperation. To the extent this experiment is carried on with conviction, India will not only benefit economically but will have made significant progress toward the global role to which, under the current distribution of powers, she has to inch her way through a judicious combination of political and economic diplomacy.

References

1. Address to UN General Assembly Special Session, November 3, 1948, cit. Dorothy Norman, *Nehru: The First Sixty Years*, vol II, p 422, Doubleday, New York, 1965.
2. UN Doc A/C/ 2/L 331, GAOR 1957 session Annexes.
3. G.A. Resoultion 2186 (XII), also GAOR session XXI, June 1966, agenda item 38, UN Doc A/C/ 2?L 910 (Annexes).
4. *Yearbook of the United Nations* 1967, p 370; ibid, 1968, p407; ibid, 1969, p 371. Also, *Report of the Secretary-General* 1970-71 GAIR XXVI session Suppl 1, UN Document A/8401.

5. See S.N. Tawale, *India's Economic Diplomacy at the United Nations*, 86-101, Meenakshi, Meerut, 1975. Also, Raul Prebisch, *Goblal Development Strategy, A Moral Responsibility*, rep.in Helene Castel (ed), *World Development*, pp 46-65, Macmillan, New York, 1971.
6. Arthur Lall, *Modern International Negotiations, Principles and Practice*, pp 203-32, New York, 1966.
7. Kamal M. Hagras, *UNCTAD, a case study in U.N. Diplomacy*, pp 91 and 134, Praeger, New York, 1965.
8. ibid.
9. *Report of the Second UNCTAD conference* (New Delhi, 1968), p 278, GOI, Ministry of Commerce, New Delhi, 1968.
10. Lok Sabha Statement April 1, 1968.
11. Report of the UNCTAD Secretary-General to 3rd Session, *The International Development Strategy, Document No TD/99*, p7.
12. Finance Minister Y.B. Chavan's address to the Committee of Twenty at Nairobi (23 September, 1973) cit. Satish Kumar (ed) *Documents on India's Foreign Policy* 1973, pp 96-97, Macmillan (India), Delhi 1976.
13. *Foreign Affairs Record*, August 1973, pp 290-300.
14. ibid. September 1973, pp 323-27.
15. ibid. November 1973, p 391.
16. Lal Bahadur Shastri, *Speeeches*, p 103, GOI, Ministry of Information and Broadcasting, New Delhi, 1965.
17. Indira Gandhi, *Speeches and Reminiscences*, p 146, Rupa, Calcutta, 1975.
18. *MEA Report* 1976-77, p 60.
19. ibid, 1975-76, pp 74 ff.
20. G.I. Chuffrin, *Economic Cooperation and Collective Security in Asia*, pp 7-8, Vikas, New Delhi, 1976; and *Ram Sharma, IFP Annual Survey* 1971, p 36.
21. GOI, *Ministry of Industrial Development, Report* 1972-73, pp 128-31, New Delhi
22. cit. Chinani, supra, p 118.
23. *Economic Times*, 16 October 1964.
24. *Indian Exporter and Importer*, July 1972, p 17 and March 1977, pp 23-26.
25. Budget speech, 23 April 1973, *Documents on India's Foreign Policy*, 1973, Satish Kumar (ed), p 41.
26. FICCI *Documents and Correspondence* 1961, p 125.
27. MEA Report 1966-67, New Delhi, 1967, p 82. For details of the reorgainsation of the Ministry and its Secretariat see K.P. Misra, *Foregin Policy and its Planning*, pp 16-44, Asia, Bombay, 1970.
28. MEA Report 1972-73, pp 75-76.
29. ibid, 1974-75, p 88.

APPENDIX I

Indian Joint Ventures Abroad

Si. No	Country	In Production	Under implementation	Approved but not yet implemented
1	2	3	4	5
1.	Afghanistan	-	3	2
2.	Australia	-	-	1
3.	Canada	1	-	2
4.	Coloumbia	-	-	1
5.	Ceylon	3	-	8
6.	Cyprus	-	1	-
7.	Dubai	-	4	-
8.	Ethiopia	2	-	5
9.	Fiji 1	1	-	
10.	Ghana	-	-	1
11.	Greneda	-	-	1
12.	Hong Kong	1	1	-
13.	Indonesia	2	6	7
14.	Iran	1	3	5
15.	Iraq	-	-	1
16.	Ireland	1	-	1
17.	Libya	-	-	1
18.	Kenya	7	1	4
19.	Lebanon	-	-	1
20.	Mauritius	3	5	3
21.	Malaysia	24	20	11
22.	Nigeria	3	1	7
23.	Nepal	-	1	-
24.	Phillippines	1	3	-
25.	Qatar	-	1	-
26.	Singapore	1	6	1
27.	SaudiArabia	-	1	3
28.	Senegal	-	-	1
29.	Thailand	3	3	1
30.	Togo	-	-	2
31.	Tanzania	-	-	3
32.	Trinidad	-	-	1
33.	Uganda	1	-	-
34.	USA	4	2	1
35.	United Kingdom	3	1	2
36.	West Germany	1	-	1
37.	YAR -	-	1	
38.	Zambia	-	2	3
Total		63	66	82

Source: *Ministry of External Affairs Reports*

APPENDIX II

Statement showing the number of Indian experts deputed to various countries under ITEC Programme (1976)

Si. No	Name of Country	Experts in position
1.	Afghanistan	124
2.	Ethiopia	2
3.	Fiji	5
4.	Ghana	3
5.	Guyana	10
6.	Indonesia	5
7.	Maldives	4
8.	Mauritius	49
9.	PDRY (Aden)	12
10.	Senegal	1
11.	Somalia	1
12.	Sri Lanka	5
13.	Tonga	2
14.	Cyprus	1
15.	Malta	3
16.	Zambia	1
17.	Barbados	1
18.	Laos	1
	Total	230

APPENDIX III

Trainees from developing countries receiving training in India (1976-77) under ITEC Programme

Si. No	Name of Country	Number
1.	Afghanistan	5
2.	Cyprus	1
3.	Ethiopia	2
4.	Ghana	1
5.	PDRY	2
6.	Maldives	12
7.	Sri Lanka	14
8.	Sudan	8
9.	Tanzania	232*
10.	Zambia	4
11.	Burma	6
12.	D.R.V.N.	16
13.	Laos	1
14.	Trinidad and Tobago	6
15.	Thailand	1
16.	Egypt	2
17.	Nigeria	4
18.	Iraq	5
19.	Zimbabwe	2
20.	Guyana	2
21.	Algeria	1
22.	Brazil	1
23.	Ecuador	1
24.	Mauritius	1
25.	Mexico	1
26.	Libya	1
27.	Zaire	1
28.	Argentina	1
	Total	340

Source: *Ministry of External Affairs Reports*

*167 of these trainees are under a grant received by Tanzania from Sweden: all the arrangements for training are, however, made by India.

6
Towards a Conclusion

In the foregoing pages an attempt has been made to depict and analyse the trends of foreign economic policies of India insofar as they follow from and, in turn, reinforce the broad principles determining the country's foreign relations and its place in the present international system as a whole. Assuming that there has not been any great divergence between the thinking and the implementation aspects of the policies, the need arises of an overall assessment of their effectiveness. Lest a contrary assumption should call in question the validity of such assessment it is important to point out that the question of implementation is one of conformity of the administrative apparatus to certain directives of the policy making authorities and is entirely outside the scope of the present enquiry. What concerns it directly is the consistency of the policies sought to be implemented in terms of the values that they are supposed to promote or reject. Another related aspect is that of their cost-effectiveness i.e. the extent to which the expected benefits outweigh any loss sustained in the process of changing the status quo and choosing a particular line instead of other available alternatives. It should be admitted, however, that any conclusion reached in these respects is at best tentative and at worst a testimony to the methodological imperfections that should be taken care of in a study like this.

Cured of rhetorics, the values that the policy makers in India have set before themselves may be enumerated and graded somewhat along these lines:

Priority	Policy Objectives
First	Territorial integrity and political independence
Second	International prominence both at regional and global level
Third	Capability to generate increasing power inputs necessary for the first two objectives

Fourth	Creation of a safe and favourable world environment
Fifth	Propagation of a world view that favours change without being radical about it.

Clearly, these are the main ingredients of the policy objectives which come under such package expression as Panch Sheel or Nonalignment. Each of these has a corresponding economic connotation which is seldom lost sight of whenever an important announcement is made, a negotiation undertaken or an agreement reached in the international sphere. Thus the maintenance of political independence and territorial integrity includes the maintenance of the philosophy and frame of the national economy as envisaged by the ruling class of the Indian society. International prominence certainly means more than mere regional leadership or prominence at global talks; it implies as well a comfortable position for Indian business interests in the world market. Similarly capability consideration apples as much to military equations with certain powers as to advantageous economic equations with many more. A safe world environment is a must for the plans of national development to be carried on undisturbed. At the same time the country needs a favourable foothold at the international bargain counters, which is why it must plead for a rule-based, new international economic order. To cap it all, there is the unmistakable concern for avoiding all sorts of ideological complications that may upset the long-term economic objectives of foreign relations.

Evidently, Indian foreign policy proceeds from three simultaneous orientations, namely, power orientation, development orientation and crisis orientation. The first, through often clouded by the moralist-idealist stance of the policy-makers, relates to the vision of a prominent position in world politics and was typically manifest in India's diplomatic involvement in the Korean and Indochinese questions as well as her activist role in the liberation of Goa or Bangladesh. If she got little tangible power advantage out the first two ventures, her title to regional superiority was more than established after the sub continental military turmoil. The third, i.e., crisis orientation is a post-colonial legacy and has almost grown into an obsession for want of comfortable relations with one or two neighbouring countries. This aspect makes it all the more imperative on the part of the authorities to take special care of the defence component of the country's foreign relations, nuclear advance not excluded. But the superstructure of power—political, military or diplomatic, needs constant support of an expanding economy which for erstwhile colonies like India means the difficult proposition of building everything anew. A development orientation therefore tops all other approaches to foreign policy and calls for clear enunciations about two major issues. The first is: what should be the role of the state in economic reconstruction, i.e., should it be that of observer, catalytic or pioneer? The second is: should it continue to rely on the existing complementarities in the external economic sphere or search for new ones?

These basic issues could not be resolved without making explicit the ideological character of the state. It is therefore significant that the principles of mixed economy at home and nonalignment abroad admirably complement each other in the efforts of the ruling forces to steer clear of the complications of an ideologically divided world. The image of development they project is charactersied by an alleged non-allegiance to either capitalism or socialism and has come to be euphemistically called the non-capitalist path. This rejection on surface of alien ideologies is clearly a concession to the susceptibilities of the national bourgeoisie who do not possess either the capacity to lay the foundations of a flourishing capitalist society primarily on their own nor the inclination to see themselves reduced to non-entities by a truly socialist state. The consensus at the national level therefore is in favour of a gradual transformation of the economy by the joint efforts of state and private enterprise with resources supplemented by foreign assistance coming from sources which may not interfere with this middle-of-the road development strategy.

The inventory of values pursued by the authorities in the sphere of foreign relations is certainly calculated to serve this consensus. Apparently there is little possibility of any great inconsistency developing in the policies for achieving these values provided the trends within and outside the domestic economy do not upset the rather precarious balance of forces on which such policies rest. As has already been noted, the business-government relations in India have developed a striking similarity of attitudes towards the questions of relations with big powers, of ensuring a steady flow of foreign capital whether in the from of aid or transnational investment, of diversifying trade and commerce with countries outside the conventional orbit and, last but not least, of patronising Indian investment in the third would countries. As a result the state is committed to do everything within its power to minimise if not entirely remove any likely conflict between the Indian and foreign business interests.

The art of balancing these interests, however, is far from self-ensuring. It is made all the more difficult as new and unforeseen stresses develop within and outside the national economy, interrupting the flow of resources in both directions. In particular demand stresses arising out of sudden or chronic shortages, say of food and fuel, equipments and know-how or arms and ammunitions may create special problems for the authorities. Unless mitigated by timely rescue coming from known quarters, these critical shortages may also force a rethinking about the rationale of existing complementarities with outside economies, as well as the strategies of development at home. Such rethinking has been forced on more than one occasion, for instance the Chinese attack in 1962, Found-Bank pressures in the wake of the Second and the Fourth Five Year Plan to deemphasize the role of public sector, IMF prescriptions for devaluation, the political uses of PL-480 food supplies or interruption thereof as a punitive measure by the USA against India's role in the Bangladesh war. The 1970s therefore saw for the first time India risking an almost direct confrontation with the USA and openly proclaiming her decision to enter into special relations with the other super power. The exigencies of the then political and military situation and the worsening economic conditions of the country combined once again to drive home the wisdom of self-reliance which had already been learned several times before. Way back in 1966 i.e. after the Indo-Pak hostilities of 1965, the Government brought out a publication on the Meaning of Self-Reliance, in which several Union Ministers waxed sentimental on the need to stand on one's own feet. Mr B.R. Bhagat wrote:

> Economic development in India since Independence has taken place within an environment of peace and security of our borders. We have been able, therefore, to undertake plans of development which involved considerable dependence on imported equipments and supplies a part of which was financed by generous foreign assistance.

> In the changed context, however, we must recognise the realities of the international situation and prepare ourselves to face the possibility of our **having to do without** substantial economic aid from abroad. The strategy of development which we have adopted so far will, therefore need to be altered.

A similar urge was felt in the wake of the Bangladesh War when self-reliance once again become the war cry on the economic front. Indeed, as has been shown in this work, several strategies have been tried with some success to reduce the country's external dependence. But the question remains: to what extent is self-reliance achievable, given the inelasticities of the country's production system and the increasing demands for certain products that must be imported in the interest of defence and development. Obviously it is a laudable idea that nothing should be done to allow foreign powers to exploit the country's internal and external crises and dictate the do's and don'ts for its economic and foreign policies. In fact therein lies the main foundation of the autonomy of decision-making in foreign affairs.

But the entire thinking about autonomy and self-reliance is likely to be misguided if no distinction was drawn between dependence and dependency. In the world of today the dependence of one nation on another cannot be entirely ruled out, although in periods of crisis dependence may constitute additional constraints on decision-making. What is more costly and may even prove to be ruinous is dependency which is a structural phenomenon. The bitterness associated with dependence is felt more acutely in times of crisis than in normal times when it is mainly a matter of accepting or rejecting the terms of dependence. Thus India's dependence on foreign sources for supply of enriched uranium is something that cannot be helped and if it means inconvenience not to get the required supply from a given sources, search must begin for alternative sources with better prospects of supply or else one must do without any import whatsoever. More injurious is the phenomenon of dependency which is characteristic of most countries colonized by the west and results in almost a perpetual bondage for them with the metropolitan power and eventually with the entire system of monopoly capital. The continuance of dependency even after the restoration of political independence of a nation is mainly attributable to the existence of a comprador and collusive bourgeoisie who habitually act as the convenient handmaid of metropolitan powers. Although in India the national bourgeoisie are believed to have attained the maturity to dislike any undue dominance of foreign capital and although they have got a special leverage on the state apparatus to fulfill their ambition, it is no good ruling out the possibility of a tripartite arrangement between the government, domestic business interests and foreign investor. It is true that the policies of the Indian government, so far have been cautiously nationalistic and have been marked by the innovation of several legal and administrative devices to keep foreign multinationals at bay. But a country which is capital-hungry and technologically backward may feel the compulsion of brining more and more foreign capital and know-how by diluting some of the safeguards against their indiscreet operation. Much of the effectiveness of the countrer-dependency drive of the authorities will therefore depend on their honesty of intentions and the quality of rapport they maintain with the more responsible sections of the business community at home.

Coming to the question of cost-effectiveness of the policies of India in the economic and political transactions with foreign nations, one thing must be squarely rejected, namely any pretension that either the cost or the benefit side of the operation of foreign policy can be measured and compared meaningfully through the application of quantitative devices. After all, in the long run, the acid test of the successes of any foreign policy is its acceptability to the people whose interests it is intended to serve. And there is considerable scope fore a debate as to the kind of people whose interests the foreign office in a particular period is really anxious to serve. For, whatever the beauty of an ambiguous notion like national interest, it ultimately boils down to the demands articulated and aggregated on behalf of the most dominant section of the society. Form that viewpoint it may be somewhat an idle guess-work if one tried to analyse the cost-benefit relation of India's foreign policy in purely general terms. It should be conceded anyway that the benefits accruing to different sections of the society considerably vary from case to case. And there is no definite knowledge so far as to the question: for whom the bell tolls?

Cost-effectiveness may however be judged in terms of the gain or loss of advantage due to the choice of a particular policy line in preference to other available alternatives. So far as India, or any post-colonial country for that matter, is concerned, the range of alternative policy lines is rather restricted. This is not only because of the global power rivalry and hegemonistic aspirations of the super power but also because of the uneven distribution of world resources. One may either continue the old subservient relations with the western world or run the risk of a complete breach, the risk being that of working out a new and, therefore, uncertain relationship with the emergent system of world socialism. Neither of these alternatives seemed to attract the ruling forces in post-independence India for the simple reason that most of the high priority policy objectives they had accepted were likely to be stifled if the final decision centre for the country's foreign policy was allowed to be shifted to one or the other foreign capital. To be fair, such a prospect was and still is an anathema to the liberal patriotic section of the national leaders. An ideological equidistance was therefore considered to be the wisest stance from which to branch forth into three exploratory directions each with a different but related mission, namely, extraction of greater advantages from the capitalist west, cultivation of a gradually expanding relationship with the socialist world not so much out of any special admiration for socialism as out of the need to ensure greater flexibility of economic diplomacy and mobilize the support of other third world countries in similar predicament.

It appears that this three-fold strategy of dealing with the outside world was intended at the outset to keep the escape doors open in case the move in a particular direction proved abortive or unrewarding. It is this calculated flexibility which largely accounts for the oft-discussed ad hocism of the Indian decision makers in the face of any hotly debated issue on the political plane. The charge leveled by the western critics that India is more non-aligned against the west than the Soviet bloc would not hold good if one realized that Indian inclination in favour of the Soviet, if there is any, is the result of her failure to evoke sufficient sympathy of the which she looks forward first before turning to the other side. And this failure has occurred not merely in respect of certain sensitive political issues such as Kashmir or Goa, China or Pakistan but more painfully in the economic sphere. Be it trade or aid, import or investment, she has had a less respectable deal, often a raw one, from the West than has been her experience with the Soviet world. After all international economic transaction more than the most engaging political confrontion can teach a nation the long term wisdom about the reliability of a particular association.

This is not to suggest that the lessons once learnt will crystalise into permanent guidelines. On the contrary the basic imperatives of industrial development in which government and business interests move hand in gloves may well compel frequent slide back into the lap of the old capitalist west. Whether this will be taking place in the true fashion of opportunist diplomacy or as a final surrender of the national bourgeoisie to the pressures of world capitalism will depend on the class composition of the ruling circles in India, their attitude to the question of social justice and their political distance from the mass at large. To date, those who have come to hold power, the old Congress, the new Congress and the Janata, share one common attribute, namely, a not too radical commitment to the economic transformation of the country so that the imperatives of development never became too overwhelming to discard the present strategy of getting the best out of a bad situation. This also explains why the philosophy of development by self-reliance has not received more than lip sympathy of the 'sharers of state power' in India, who cannot simply think of doing it all on their own. External linkage, therefore, will be diversified and mended where necessary but never discarded or restructured in a substantial manner.

There remains the third line of strategy, called 'interdeveloping' with the other less developed countries, which is likely to further influence the attitude of the ruling circles towards the economic bases of foreign policy. It has been argued in this work that the common front forged by India with the non-aligned countries and more recently with the Group of 77 is likely to bring rich dividends, political as well as economic if one considered the great need of the country for the necessary support to confront the developed world with an array of demands for justice not only for its own sake but for others as well. At the same time, the excellent opportunity it brings to the Indian bourgeoisie to expand their business into new and promising areas may lead to a significant alignment of the rising capitalist forces in the third world. That this new found solidarity may cut both ways should be obvious to any discerning observer of public affairs. On the one hand, it will strengthen the world position of the Indian decision makers; on the other, it may confront them with an hitherto unknown crisis, which is likely to unfold itself in the course of time if the operations of Indian business abroad, particularly the joint ventures run in collaboration with foreign business capital, enter into rough weather and are wrongly or rightly looked upon as frustrating local development. Though every effort is expected to be made to arrest such an untoward happening, the implications of the eventuality especially the strains it would create for India's position in the third world cannot be underestimated.

The crossroads lying ahead therefore will be of great uncertainty although they will have been reached via the path of least resistance, compromise and adjustment. It is at these crossroads that the vow of self-reliance will be tested and the fate of the autonomy of decision making will be settled. As far as one can foresee now, the political economy of India is yet to develop those crucial strains which may precipitate reaching the crossroads. But any major economic calamity at home or a sudden collapse of the present international balance of forces of the Capitalist, Non-Capitalist and Socialist affiliation would certainly hasten the prospect.

Select Bibliography

Almond, Gabriel and Coleman, James: Politics of the Developing Areas, Princeton University 1960.

Aron, Raymond: Peace and War: A Theory of International Relations, Doubleday, Garden City, New York 1966.

Bandopadhyay, J: The Making of India's Foreign Policy, Allied, Calcutta 1978.

Baran, PA and Sweezy, PM: Monopoly Capital, Monthly Review Press New York 1966.

Best, Michael H and Connally William E: The Politicized Economy, DC Heath, Laxington 1976.

Bhagawati, JN and Srinivasan, TN: Foreign Trade and Economic Development of India, North Holland Pub., Amsterdam 1974.

Bhatia, OP: The Role of Multinationals in India, Asian Labour No 116, February 1975.

Bijli, Shah M: Developing Nations and UNCTAD, International Book, Aligarh 1973.

Bornschier, V: Cross-national Evidence of the Effects of Foreign Investment, *American Journal* of Sociology, November 1978.

Breacher, Michael: India and World Politics, OUP, London 1968.

__________ Nehru: A Political Biography , OUP, London 1959.

Brutents, K: A Historical View of Neo-Colonialism, Novosti, Moscow 1972.

Caporaso, James A: Dependence and Dependency in the Global System, *International Organisation*, vol 32 No 1 1972.

Chandra, KN: World Imperialism, *Economic & Political Weekly,* February 1973.

Chhabra, HS (ed): *Indian Economic Diary,* New Delhi (prog).

Chinani, Babubhai M: India's March to Democratic Socialism, Brihad Bharatiya Samaj, Bombay 1972.

Chuffirin, GT: Economic Cooperation and Collective Security in Asia, Vikas, New Delhi 1976.

Communist Party of India: Calcutta Party Congress Statements, CPI, New Delhi, 1948.

Cottam, Richard L: Foreign Policy Motivations, Pittsburgh Univ. 1977.

Crabb, Cecil V: The Testing of Non-alignment, *Western Political Qly* Vol 17, September 1964

Das, Durga: India: From Curzon to Nehru and After, Collins, London 1969.

Dasgupta, J: Season of Caesars: Emergency Regime and India, *Asian Survey,* April 1978.

Datta, Bhabatosh: Private Sector and the National Planing Process in R.C. Dutt and RK Nigam (ed) Toward Commanding Heights, SCOP, New Delhi 1975.

Dutta, Subimal:With Nehru in the Foreign Office, Minerva, Calcutta 1977.

Elliott, William Y: The Political Economy of American Foreign Policy, H.Holt, New York 1955.

Federation of Indian Chambers of Commerce: Correspondence and Relevant Documents, New Delhi (Prog).

__________ Fortnightly Review, New Delhi (Prog).

__________ Report on Indian Recession, New Delhi 1966.

Frankel, Francine R: India's Political Economy, Macmillan (NY) 1977.

Fulbright, William J: The Arrogance of Power, Random, New York 1966.

Galbraith, JK: Ambassador's Journal, Hughton-Miffin Boston 1969.
Galtung, Johan: Structural Theory of Imperialism, Journal of Peace Research No. 2, 1971.
Gandhi, Indira: Speeches and Reminiscences, Rupa, Calcutta 1975.
Ghosh, Ajoy: Communist Answer to Pandit Nehru, CPI, New Delhi.
Gilpin, Robert: Political Economy of Multinational Corporations, *American Political Science Review* March 1976.
__________US Power and the MNC, Macmillan, New York 1975.
Government of India——Dept of Company Affairs, Company News & Notes, Delhi (Prog).
——Dept of Economic Affairs: India and International Monetary Reforms, New Delhi 1975.
Government of India ____Directorate of Technical Development, Report on Foreign Collaborations, New Delhi 1974.
____Ministry of External Affairs, Annual Reports, New Delhi (Prog).
——of Finance, Annual Report, Economic Survey, New Delhi (Prog).
——of Industries, Annual Report, New Delhi (Prog).
——Parliament Sectt, Constituent Assembly Debates, Fariadabd, 1966.
__________ Estimates Committee Report on Utilisation of External Assistance, New Delhi 1967-68.
——Planning Commission, Five Year Plans, Plan Resources and Outlay, New Delhi 1959.
——Press Information Bureau, Press Notes on Industrial Policy, February 1973.
Gupta, Bhupesh: 25 Years of Independence, CPI, New Delhi 1972.
Gupta, KR: Working of State Trading Corporation in India, S Chand, New Delhi 1970.
Gupta, Sulekh Chandra: Freedom From Foreign Food, Blitz, New Delhi 1965.
Gupta, Vinod (ed): Anderson Papers, New Delhi 1972.
Gyan Chand: Nehru and Planning in Nehru Legacy, National Book Club, New Delhi 1966.

Hagras, Kamal M: UNCTAD: A Case Study in UN Diplomacy, Praeger, New York 1965.
Halder, Animesh: India's Export Pattern, Minerva, Calcutta 1976.
Halder and Richard: Structural Characteristics of Indian Foreign Aid, *Indian Economic Jnl* Vol 21 No 2 October 1973.
Hayter, Teresa: Aid as Imperialism, Penguin M'Sex 1971.
Hazari, RK: Foreign Collaboration, Bombay University 1967.
Heenan, David A and Keegan WJ: The Rise of Third World Multinationals, *Harvard Business Review*, Jan-Feb 1979.
Higginbotham: In the Wake of Bangaldesh, *Pacific Affairs* Vol 54 No 3.
Hymer, A: Inernational Politics and International Economics: A Radical View, *Monthly Review* Vol 29 March 1978.
Horowitz, Irving: Three Worlds of Development, OUP, New York 1966.

Iengar, HVR: Business and Planned Economy, Vora, Bombay 1968.

Jacobs, Norman (ed): Making Foreign Policy in a Nuclear Age, FPA, New York 1963.
Jalee, Pierre: The Pillage of the Third World, Monthly Review Press, New York 1968.
Johnson, Lyndon B: The Vantage Point, Holt, Rinehart & Winston, New York 1971.

Kapur, Ashok: Emerging Pattern of India's Foreign Policy, *Foreign Affairs Reporter* Vol 20 No 7.
Kidron, Michael: Foreign Investment in India, London 1965.
Kothari, Rajni: Indian Foreign Policy: Need for a Non-doctrinnaire Perspective in AB Shah (ed) India's Defence and Foreign Policy, Manaktalas, Bombay 1963.
Kumar, Satish: Documents on India's Foreign Policy (1973 and 1974), Macmillian, India 1976.

Lall, Arthur: Modern International Negotiations: Principles & Practice, New York 1961.
Lall, KB: Nehru and International Cooperation in BR Nanda (ed) Indian Foreign Policy: Nehru Years, Vikas, New Delhi 1976.
Lall, Sanjay: Developing Countries and Emerging International Technological Order, Inl of International Affairs, Spring 1979.
La Palombra JG and Blank Stephen: Multinational Corporations in Comparative Perspective.
Lipton, Michael and Firm, John: The Erosion of Relations Between India and Britain, RIIA, OUP, London 1975.
Little and Clifford: International Aid, Allen and Unwin, London 1965.
Levy, Walter: A Warning to Oil-importing Nations, *Fortune*, May 21, 1979.
Lewin, Pauline: The Foreign Trade of Communist China, Praeger, New York 1964.
Lyon, Peter: India's Foreign Policy, *South Asian Studies* Vol 4 No 1.

Magdoff, Harry: The Age of Imperialism, Monthly Review Press New York 1969.
Mahajani, Usha: India and Southeast Asia, *United Asia*, May-June 1970.
Malenbaum, Wilfred: East and West in India's Development, NPA, USA 1959.
Mansergh, Nicholas: Documents and Speeches on British Commonwealth Affairs, RIIA, OUP, London 1953.
Maprail, Cyriac: Nehru and the Commonwealth, Radiant, New Delhi 1976.
Mcfarlane, B: Imperialism in 1980s, *Journal of Contemporary Aisa*, Vol 7 No 4.
Mende, Tybor: Nehru, George Brazillier, New York 1956.
Menon, R: India and Soviet Union, *Asian Survey*, June 1978.
Mehta, Balraj: Foreign Aid and Indian Economy ,*Indian Left Review*, Vol 4 No 1 October 1975.
Merritt, Richard L: Communications in International Politics, Illinois University, Urbana 1972.
Misra, Girish: Public Sector in India's Economy, CPI, New Delhi 1975.
Misra, KP (ed): Foreign Policy of India: A Book of Readings, Thomson Press, New Delhi 1977
__________Foreign Policy and its Planning, Asia, Bombay 1970.
__________International Politics in the Indian Ocean, *Orbis*, Vol 18, Winter 1975.
Modelski, George: A Theory of Foreign Policy, Praeger, New York 1962.
__________ Transnational Corporation and World Order, Subarnarekha, Calcutta 1978.
Mukherjee, R: Economics of Soviet Trade and Aid, Freeman, Sanfrancisco 1979.
Myrdal, Gunnar: An International Economy, Harper, New York 1969.

National Council of Applied Economic Research, Export Strategy for India, New Delhi 1969.
Nayyar, Baldevraj: The Modernization Imperative and Indian Planning, Vikas, New Delhi 1972.
Nayyar, Deepak (ed): Economic Relations Between the Socialist Countries and the Third World, Macmillan, London 1967.
Nehru, Jawaharlal: India's Foreign Policy, Govt. of India Publications Div. New Delhi 1961.
_________ Visit to America: Speeches, Johan Day, New York 1950.
_________ Speeches (Vol I & II), GOI, New Delhi.
Nizami, Taufiq Ahmed: The Communist Party and India's Foreign Policy, Associated, New Delhi 1971.
Noreng, Oystern: Oil Politics in the 20th Century, (Council on Foreign Relation Inc.) Mcgraw Hill, New York 1978.
Nye. JS and Mark, CJ: Independence and Interdependence, *Foreign Policy* No 22 and 24, 1976.

O.E.C.D. Development Cooperation, Review, Paris 1973.
_________ Report of President, Paris (prog).

Panglaykin, J and Palmer, Ingrid: State Trading Corporation in Developing Countries, Rotterdam Univ. 1969.
Patel, IG: Foreign Aid, Allied, Bombay 1968.
———— New International Economic Order, *Eastern Economist* Vol 63, No 5.
Pavlov, VI (ed): Asia and Africa: Fundamental Changes, USSR Academy of Sciences, Novosti Moscow 1972.
Payer, Cheryl: The Debt Trap, Monthly Review Press, New York 1974.
Power, Paul: On Ideologies in India's Foreign Policy, *Indian Pol Sc Rev.* Vol 8 No 1.
Prasad, Bimla: The Orgins of Indian Foreign Policy, Bookland, New Delhi 1962.
Prebisch, Raul: Global Development Strategy in Helen Castel (ed) World Development Macmillan, New York 1971.

Rajan, MS: India World Politics, *International Jnl,* Toronto 1968.
Range, William: Jawaharlal Nehru: World View, Geogia Univ, Athena 1981.
Ranis, Gustav: The United States and Developing Economics, New York 1964.
Ray, Ajit: Sharers in India's State Power in M.Kurian (ed) India: State & Society, Orient Longman, Bombay 1975.
Reinhardt, JM: Foreign Policy and National Integration, Yale Univ., New Haven 1971.
Reserve Bank of India: Bulletins, Bombay (prog).
________ Foreign Collaboration in Indian Industries: Survey, Bombay 1968 and 1970.
________ Financial Statics of Joint Stock Compaines, Bombay 1978.
________Report on Currency and Finance, Bombay (prog).
________Survey of India's Foreign Liabilities and Assets, Bombay 1958.
________Report of Study Group on Nonbanking Companies, Bombay 1975.
Robbins, Lionel Charles: Political Economy: Past and Present, Columbia Univ., New York 1976.
Rosecrance Richard and Stein, Arthur: Interdependence: Myth or Reality, *World Politics* Vol 26 No 1 October 1973.
Russett, Bruce M: World Handbook of Political and Social Indicators, Yale Univ., New Haven 1964.

Schlesinger, James R: The Political Economy of National Security, Praeger, New York 1960.
Schumpeter, Joseph: Imperialism and Social Class, Meridian, New York 1955.
Shenoy, BR: The Sterling Assets of Reserve Bank of India, ICWA, New Delhi 1946.
Silverstein, Harvey B: The 22nd General Assembly: Issues and Alignments, Arizona Univ., 1971.
Sigmund, Paul E (ed): The Ideology of Developing Nations, Praeger, New York 1972.
Singh, Ram et al. Kennedy through Indian Eyes, Vir Pub, Delhi 1964.
Smith BLR: The New Political Economy: the Public and the Private Sector, Macmillan, London 1975.
Snyder, Richard C (ed): Foreign Policy Decisionmaking, Free Press, New York 1962.
Srivastava, PK: Foreign Collaboration, Shivlal, Agra 1974.
Stanislaus, M.Sebastian: Soviet Economic Aid to India, NV Publication, New Delhi 1975.
Strange, Susan: International Economic Relations in Roger Morgan (ed) The Study of International Affairs, RIIA, OUP, London 1972.
Sullivan, James: Reorientation of India's Arms Control Policy, *Asian Survey* Vol 13 No 7.

Tata Services Ltd: Statistical Outline of India, Bombay (prog).
Tawale, SN: India's Economic Diplomacy at the United Nations, Meenakshi, Meerut 1975.
Thornton, RC: Imbalance on the Subcontinent, *Orbis,* Fall 1975.
Tyson, Geoffrey: India and the Russian Visitors, International Affairs RIIA, OUP, London 1956.

UN CTAE: Gatt Declarations, Final Act and Documents, Havana 1948.
UNCTAD: Report of Conferences (I to V).
UNCTAD Secretary General: The International Development Strategy, New York 1972.
United Nations: Multinational Corporation in World Development, New York 1973.
__________ Yearbook, New York (prog).
__________ General Assembly Official Records, New York (prog).
United Nations: Statistical Yearbook, New York (prog).
United Nations: Texts of Conventions and Other Instruments concerning International Trade Law, New York 1971.
UN ECAFE: Foreign Trade Statistics for Asia and Far East, (prog).
US Government: Public Papers of the Presidents (Truman to Nixon),USGPO, Washington D.C.
__________ Congressional Records.
__________ Senate and House Committee Reports.

Varma, Yogendra P: Growth of Protectionism in India, S.Chand, New Delhi 1974.
Vartikar, VS: Commercial Policy and Economic Development in India , Praeger, New York 1969.
Venu, S: The Developing Economies and International Framework, Orient Longman, Bombay 1971.
Vital, David: The Inequality of States, OUP, Oxford 1967.

Ward, Barbara: The Rich Nations and the Poor Nations, Norton, New York 1962.
Weintrabb, S: North-South Dialogue, *International Affairs* April 1977.

Zakaria, Raflq (ed): A Study of Nehru, *Times of India*, Bombay 1959.

Index